C000226944

Nearness of Ice

ARCTIC CONVOYS

Collated by Kate Newmann

for Arnie,
whose grandfather knew —

love
Kate

July 2022

First published in 2016 by

The Pushkin Trust and The Arts Council of Northern Ireland

LOTTERY FUNDED

© Individual authors

Printed by Nicholson & Bass Ltd.

A catalogue record for this book is available from the British Library

ISBN 978-1-909751-63-7

This book is printed on elemental chlorine-free paper

FSC
Mixed Sources
Product group from well-managed
forests, controlled sources and
recycled wood or fibre

Cert no. SGS-COC-005221
www.fsc.org
© 1996 Forest Stewardship Council

Foreword

IN OCTOBER 2014 I had the honour to be present at the Harbour Commission in Belfast when sixteen seamen from Northern Ireland were presented with the Ushakov Medal on behalf of the Russian Federation by the Russian Ambassador, Dr Alexander Yakovenko.

It was a most moving occasion to witness these courageous men being recognised for their extraordinary bravery and who by supporting Russia along with the Allied Forces in the Second World War, succeeded in defeating the peril of Nazism.

I felt that their story should be shared and immortalised in a book and I am particularly delighted that the noted poet and writer, Kate Newmann has compiled their stories into this book, *Nearness of Ice*, that will live on for ever.

I believe that their story exemplifies the power of human solidarity to overcome the axis of evil and how against all odds what is true triumphs in the end.

The Duchess of Abercorn
Honorary Consul to the Russian Federation in Northern Ireland
Founder, Pushkin Trust

THE STORY OF the Arctic convoys brings together two of the epic narratives of the 20th Century – firstly, the global struggle against the Nazis and, secondly but simultaneously, that against the forbidding ice-storms of the northern oceans.

The expeditions from Britain to the top of the world between 1941 and 1945, to Murmansk and Archangelsk, in support of the Russian allies against Hitler, were journeys no less tremendous for being so sustained, so perilous and so persistent.

This – in so many ways – 'silent' war, fought far from the conventional zones of European conflict and, by necessity, in great secrecy, of course still produced its heavy and melancholy catalogue of loss of life and injury, visible and invisible, among what were overwhelmingly Merchant Navy seamen.

The critical and often-overlooked heroism of these sailors was recognised in 2014 by the Russian Government with the award of the Ushakov Medal. Now, this small but valuable book, with its modest and sometimes shocking reflections on the campaign by surviving veterans in Northern Ireland, makes its own important contribution to the recovery and re-discovery of those days of unimaginable endurance and, it must be said, adventure.

The book also reinforces the peculiar power of the written word faced with extremity, adroitly managed with care towards all, to capture the drama of experience even among people for whom remembering and writing are difficult and fraught adventures in themselves. As a guide, listener and kind of translator, the men of the convoys, whose stories are so vividly enacted here, could have had no better than the poet Kate Newmann.

This volume is a tribute to her skills, happily also to the flexibility of Arts Council funding in being able to respond to inventive proposals such as this from Pushkin Trust, and, of course, to the survivors, the elders, whose variety of acts of remembering and retelling these pages evoke, salting away more tales, more accounts of the improbable made possible, into the common heritage of our shared culture.

Damian Smyth
Head of Literature & Drama
Arts Council of Northern Ireland

Preface

I T SEEMED a straightforward and worthwhile task – when I was invited to interview the surviving veterans of the Arctic Convoys from Northern Ireland, and produce a book. The men had attended a ceremony in Belfast where they were presented by the Russian Ambassador, Dr Alexander Yakovenko, with the Ushakov Medal, and they were so impressive on that occasion – their experiences so remarkable – that it was felt the world should know more about them. As the letter to the Arts Council of Northern Ireland stated:

These men are unrepresented in the narrative of Northern Ireland and in the narrative of the Second World War, so topical at this time of commemorations.

The idea was fascinating. My mind swam with metaphors and questions –

> *Do you dream of ocean?*
> *What did you feel about the Cold War when you'd already been*
> *in a 'cold' war?*
> *What was your rapport with weather?*
> *Does hardship melt from the mind?*
> *Do you ever really come ashore?*
> *What about whales? Barnacle geese?*
> *The song of sonar?*
> *The music of ice?*
> *The voice in the tongues of glaciers?*

Early into my research, I encountered complications. I am not a military historian, and I realised I had huge tracts of ignorance – whole languages in which I was utterly illiterate: the language of naval ranks, different in the Merchant and Royal Navies; the type and class of ships (destroyers, corvettes, aircraft carriers, cruisers, light cruisers, frigates, Crown Colony Class, Shakespeare Class, Flower Class, Town Class… stone frigate, which is a shore establishment); the parts of ships (the fo'c's'le, the galley, the bulkhead, the fiddley, hatch derricks, stern gland, pavannes); the terminology of aircraft and of weapons (Tiger Moths, Wellington Bombers, Barracuda dive-bomber, Junkers Ju-88 with screamers, GNAT torpedoes, Oerlikons); the geography (Western Approaches, Straits of Pantelleria), and the acronyms (CW – Commission Warrant, OOW – Officer of the Watch, LDV – Home Guard, CAM – Catapult Armed Merchant, HO ratings – Hostility Only, ACO – Admiralty Compass Observatory, HF/DF – High Frequency Detection Finding, ASDIC – Anti-Submarine Detection Indicators).

A visit to HMS Caroline, the ship now converted to a Naval Museum in the Titanic Quarter of Belfast, brought a reminder that careless use of the words was not an option: there is a recording there of a Naval Officer berating the men who were sloppy with their turn of phrase; who talked about 'tying up' the ship instead of 'hoving to'. To stand on the deck of HMS Caroline was salutary. A 4.5 inch gun, which sounds nominal enough, is a huge cannon-like weapon – the 4.5 inches referring to just the diameter of the large shells (as long as your forearm) that were fired from it.

I visited the Imperial War Museum in London, where a torpedo (or tin fish) takes up most of the floor of one whole exhibition space.

It was chilling – the sheer scale of the metal bomb that would have hurtled towards the body of a ship.

Part of the WWII exhibition at the Imperial War Museum includes recordings and archive footage from D-Day. It struck me as ironic that one soldier described how all the men on his landing craft were violently seasick on the approach to the beach, while the officer in charge said *one or two of the men felt a little jippy*. This discrepancy, or at least, this difference in perspective, informs the books written about the convoys. There are military histories, like *The Murmansk Venture* by Major-General Sir C. Maynard, and Admiral Schofield's *Arctic Convoys*, immersed in a language of strategy and manoeuvre, and then there are more personal responses like Sam McAughtry's *Kenbane Head*, though even he speaks of the 'tonnage' that went down. Seminal histories of the Arctic Convoys, like that by Richard Woodman, are so dense, so intent on conveying every aspect of the phenomenon that the people – the living men on board the ships – inadvertently get lost. The poet Alice Oswald recently published a new translation of Homer's *Iliad*. She says she was motivated by a desire to restore the focus, not on one main hero, but to give credence to 'the little biographies of the soldiers that crop up throughout the *Iliad*.' It seemed an emphasis which suited this project. We were blessed with having survivors / veterans / witnesses living among us, and theirs is the narrative at the core.

Alan Bennett says *It is just as well childhood happens to us at the beginning of our lives, because if it happened in the middle, we would never survive it.* The Arctic Convoys began in August 1941, less than two months after Germany invaded Russia. Inevitably, the men who contribute their stories here were very young when they sailed to North Russia, and this probably protected them to some extent. At least they were not of a high enough rank at that age, to be faced with the sort of horrendous decisions depicted in Alistair Maclean's novel *HMS Ulysses* – trying to measure which course of action will kill fewest people, or having to follow orders when they could see the lethal consequences of doing so.

But as one man, who was reluctant to meet me, said, *It was a long time ago. I'll be ninety-seven next month. I don't think I'll bother.* What right had I to foist myself into people's homes and force, or even encourage them to re-enter the past; their sometimes traumatic past experiences, especially since the psyche is so intertwined with physical well-being? As Damian Smyth, Head of Literature and Drama of the Arts Council put it – 'to haul people back for a good quotation'. In

Gabriel Garcia Marquez's factual novel *The General in His Labyrinth*, Simon Bolivar asks his nephew Fernando to write Bolivar's memoir: 'Fernando would live to the age of eighty-eight without writing anything more than a few disordered pages, for fate granted him the immense good fortune of losing his memory.'

It had been of special interest to me how men who had sailed across such vast distances and seen such far shores, could come back to Northern Ireland and fit their mental maps to the particular divided society of here. But I had forgotten, that in the context of a society where any military activity was dangerously contentious, it was bound to add an extra layer of silence. I'd forgotten too the familiar and inevitable uneasiness about having a stranger come to the house and ask questions, though the regard in which the Duchess of Abercorn is held, made my path much easier.

There is, studied in American Universities, a subject called the Aesthetic of Reticence. There was bound to be reticence. Those who had made the Navy their career have a built-in, professional reticence. There was the drummed-into-us-at-school fear of giving the wrong answer, or saying something inaccurate for the record. There was the noble self-effacement which characterised the men, and led them to understate their odysseys. There was a reticence on my part – a tentativeness around the delicate nature of commemoration. One of the veterans who had watched a documentary about the tragic PQ17 Arctic Convoy, said it was a load of rubbish. In deconstructing the myths we need to be careful.

There was the nature of memory itself: what the self, the subconscious, the conscious, chooses to jettison - what remains. At first it seemed easier to talk about D-Day, and I wondered if memory was affected by physical cold, or whether a lack of due recognition reinforced areas of forgetting.

I did not use a tape recorder, which I feared would be intrusive. I realised, talking to the men, that my questions were misguided. I was striving for – if not some answer, then some conformity, some pattern, as though, if I elicited the right response, we could, between us, crack some Enigma Code to reveal the past. My notes are at times cryptic – and I found I had invented a new inscrutable language of hasty scribbles, whereby *ac* could stand for aircraft, or arctic convoys, or actually or action stations. Transcribing and typing the notes, it is sometimes evident that the conversation had a natural lull, an organic end – and that I have persisted, like a visitor who doesn't know when to leave. But I found all the men tolerant, generous with their time, their welcome, and their energy.

Some of the narratives which came to me are posthumous. Sometimes the veterans themselves had given a recorded interview, or had written their experience at some point in the past, and this had been cared-for and kept by family members. Sometimes the memories were told to me through the families – thus being both at one remove and yet enriched by the contemplative regard of a younger generation. In many instances, families had undertaken valuable research, following up times and places – in one case tracing the name of the Commander of the U-boat which had attacked his father's ship. I am moved by the fact that this source material was placed so completely at my disposal. In the desire to be fair, given space restrictions, I had to be severely selective in terms of the text put in my care. This book in no way means to preclude the publication of individual stories. Nor is it comprehensive. Many many men served in the Royal and Merchant Navy in the Arctic Circle, who are not recorded here. An expansive archive of interviews with WWII veterans is kept in the Somme Heritage Centre, Newtownards.

Because of time restraints (the funding body required the book to be published in 2016) I was unable to give each contributor a proof copy. I assure you that I have not altered the text, other than in a few instances, to excise something which was deeply personal. The live interviews are all the more powerful because they have not been ordered into the form of an essay, but have the spontaneous rhythm of communication. In some instances I was able to make two visits, at the risk of repetition, and I have not merged these, but kept them separate.

Memory is such a mysterious phenomenon. It has its own codes of truth, and its own terms of reference and of relevance. It is in this spirit that the narratives were gathered. I felt it was more than an exercise in collecting facts. The recounting embraced all the senses and sensibilities, and people's words have been included largely unchanged. Though the impetus for this book grew from an interest in the Ushakov Medal and the connections with Russia, the oceans are not bounded in the mind, and so stories about experiences in the Atlantic, the Mediterranean, the Pacific – are included here along with revelations about the Arctic Convoys, and indeed, stories about family, about childhood, about home – since these are what define the men who went to sea at a very young age.

All the narratives are characterised by wit and compassion, and I feel privileged to have met such fine, dignified, intelligent men whose life-force is enviable. It is right and proper that their experiences are recorded in this book for everybody to read, and for us all to feel immensely proud.

I am grateful to Frank Ormsby, Jim Shaughnessy, Mike Cawthorne, Jeanette and Wilson Tosh, Richard Parkinson, Theo

Dorgan, Aidan McElwhinney, Paula Meehan, Mel McMahon, Angus Adamson, Roisin McDonagh, Laura Sloan of Windsor Graphics and to the complete empathy and co-operation of Don Hawthorn and David Anderson at Nicholson & Bass. Crucial were Damian Smyth's conviction that this book needed to come to light now, whatever was necessary to facilitate that, and the Duchess of Abercorn's desire to honour in a meaningful way, the veterans of the Arctic Convoys.

Ultimately, I am deeply indebted to the families of these veterans and to the amazing men themselves.

Kate Newmann

Contents

Introduction

ON 9TH AUGUST 1942, a grand banquet was planned in the famous Astoria Hotel in Leningrad. Adolf Hitler was to celebrate his victory over the city which had obsessed him. Leningrad, with its architecture, its grandeur, its art, its cultural institutions, the broad Neva River, seemed to him more impressive than Vienna, than Berlin. He was determined that the city be his, even if this meant decimating it. So sure was he of success, that he set the date for the victory celebrations well in advance, and it is rumoured that he actually planned the menu and printed invitation cards for 9th August 1942.

Although Adolf Hitler and Josef Stalin had signed a non-aggression pact with each other in 1939, by which they carved up Poland between them, Hitler had decided that a swift invasion of Russia was the necessary next step in his plan to make Germany great again, by expanding eastwards at the same time as westwards. As well as Jews, Hitler hated Slavs and Bolsheviks, and this is what informed the nature of that invasion. On 21st June 1941, in Operation Barbarossa, three million German soldiers were unleashed into Russia. In his desire to exterminate whole swathes of human beings, Hitler had issued Criminal Orders, which gave those soldiers not just the licence, but the instruction to murder civilians, including children, in whatever way was most efficient.

I met a woman in Vyborg, who described being a child when the Germans arrived in Belarus: *The Fascists gathered all the adults in front of the children and shot them...not dead...an arm, a leg...then they did other things, then killed them. The children had to dig a trench to put the bodies in. The soldiers just did everything... The children became adults very quickly....*

St. Petersburg is far enough north that around the summer solstice you can read a book through the night – just a faint dimming comes across the page for a short while, but not enough to darken out the print. Into the middle of these White Nights came the news, on 22nd June 1941, that Germany was at war with Russia. By 8th September 1941, St. Petersburg (then named Leningrad) was under siege.

Among the residents of Leningrad at this time, the poet Anna Akhmatova and the composer Dmitri Shostakovich, having been suppressed by Stalin, were now being asked to turn their creativity towards a patriotic rousing of the people, who were beginning to suffer greatly because of lack of food and fuel. Long after the entire principal Leningrad Philharmonic Orchestra had been taken to safety, Shostakovich was still in his war-ravaged city, speaking on the radio and writing his 7th Symphony. Akhmatova describes this composition:

As if the first thunderstorm were singing.
Or as if all the flowers broke into words.

The winter of 1941 was very severe. Eleni, Peter Ustinov's friend and his guide when he visited St. Petersburg, remembers her grandmother using their best carpet in which to wrap the body of her son, Eleni's uncle, because the ground was too frozen to bury the dead. The trams, which had frozen in situ, were crammed with corpses. And when the first thaw came, it revealed horrors which defy expression.

Shostakovich's symphony was completed after the composer, like Akhmatova, had been evacuated, and the score was smuggled back into Leningrad in March 1942, when the situation was dire. In two marvellous articles in the *Guardian*, Ed Vulliamy describes the unlikely and remarkable performance of this symphony in the besieged city.

It is impossible to comprehend a million people in one city dying of starvation. But when Edith Katya Matus took her oboe to a neighbour to get it fixed, he was lying covered in blankets with his door open. He agreed to help, but *he asked me to get him a cat or a dog – there were no cats or dogs left in the city.* People were even eating carpenter's glue and wallpaper off the walls.

Edith needed the oboe because she was joining the performance of Shostakovich's new symphony by the Leningrad Radio Orchestra. *Of an orchestra of one hundred people, there were only fifteen left…I didn't recognise the musicians…they were like skeletons…It was evident we couldn't play anything, we could hardly stand on our feet…the trumpeter didn't have the breath to play his solo.* The players suffered from the 'cold-in-heat' associated with starvation. *…Sometimes, people just fell over onto the floor while they were playing.* The orchestra was supplemented with Russian soldiers who came from the trenches, just for the duration of rehearsals, before returning to duty. No one was permitted to be late, or to miss a rehearsal – not even if they were at their wife's funeral. *We rehearsed every day except Sunday… They gave us a little extra food in the canteen of the Pushkin Theatre. Not really soup, more water with a few beans in it, and a teaspoon of wheatgerm.*

On the night of the performance, the lights above the stage went on. *I'll never forget that – I'd forgotten what electric light was like. It was more like a ceremony than a concert…* The music was broadcast on the radio, and loudspeakers blasted it towards the German soldiers. The Russian army (their equipment and munitions severely depleted) later claimed that they had launched a massive fusillade the night before, to ensure that there would be no activity from the German artillery. At any rate, *For the first time in months there was silence...Eliasberg lifted his baton, and we began... ...In apartments rising from empty streets, and along frontline trenches dug cheek-by-jowl with the invading army, citizens and soldiers clustered around radio sets. Even the Germans were listening. Afterward, it was still the city under siege, but I knew it would live.*

It was 9th August 1942 – the exact date on which Hitler had planned his banquet.

This is the context in which Winston Churchill made a promise of support to Russia and the Russian people. These were the circumstances under which Stalin was to put pressure on Churchill to keep his original promises. This was the backdrop against which Churchill, sometimes in total opposition to the Admiralty's own feelings, insisted that the Arctic Convoys should sail. And this is the reason that the men in this book sailed to North Russia, in convoys laden with tanks, aircraft, trucks, tractors, railway engines, aluminium, medical supplies, fuel and food.

Almost all of these supplies had been sent from America, carried on ships across the Atlantic, which was also a very dangerous undertaking, especially if ships had a solo passage. There were fewer losses if they sailed in groups, in formation – in convoys, with Royal Naval warships protecting the merchant vessels.

When Stalin put pressure on Roosevelt, who in turn put pressure on Churchill, it left him with a huge dilemma in regard to the aid to North Russia:

My own feeling is mingled with much anxiety...[but]
...the operation is justified...if a half gets through...

What this mathematics of war meant was men

...Making haste to that grey chessboard of ocean, on whose invisible
Squares ship related
The possible to the impossible.

Alan Ross

We have no conception of what it was that these young men (some as young as seventeen) had to contend with. We have no real knowledge of cold. As Sara Wheeler says, even after a night in her thermal tent, she had frost on her eyelashes; Colin Thubron in Siberia, in a desire to keep whatever warmth his body had generated, put on all his clothes and found he couldn't get through his narrow doorway, and Ranulph Fiennes describes the condition Arctic Eye – 'the feeling of sharp grit moving about under the lids.' The poet Alan Ross had experienced the Arctic Convoys:

The cold seen almost as a colour
– ice-grey, gelatinous, glass-edged –

Alan Ross

A week out of Iceland, nosing the Barents Sea,
And guns were trained hourly to prevent freezing...

Alan Ross

The danger from the elements meant that there was less threat from the enemy – freezing fog, ice forming on everything, ferocious storm:

> *...the sea curdles and sprawls,*
> *Liverishly real, horizon and water tilting into walls.*

Alan Ross

These were terrifying conditions and even interfered with the ships' detection equipment and signalling, but German aircraft and submarines were also affected, and less likely to attack from their bases on the Norwegian coast.

And then there was the waiting time:

> *The light is watery, like the light of the sea-bed*
> *Marooned in it, stealthy as fishes, we may even be dead.*

Alan Ross

The sea-bed is where you did not want to go. Into the sea is where you did not want to go: heavy metal debris; the suckage of a sinking ship; your heavy clothing saturated; your skin covered in thick black oil; oil burning on the water threatening to suffocate; the water itself below freezing – a lethal oxymoron of burning ice and freezing fire. The men saw that no swimming lessons could have prepared them for this. And even if they choose not to speak of it

> *...they won't forget*
> *The confusion and the oily dead ...*

Alan Ross

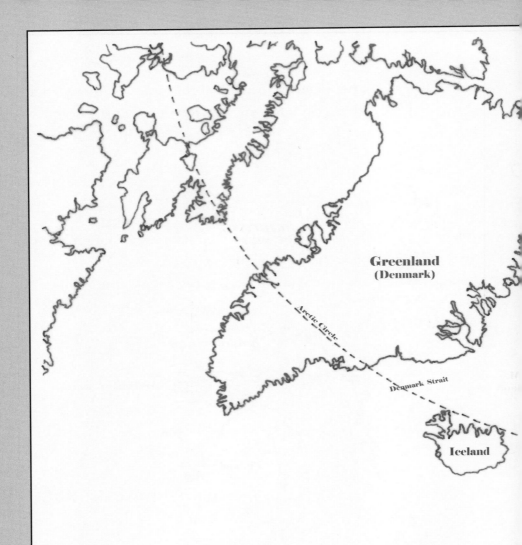

Greenland
(Denmark)

Arctic Circle

Denmark Strait

Iceland

NORTH
ATLANTIC
OCEAN

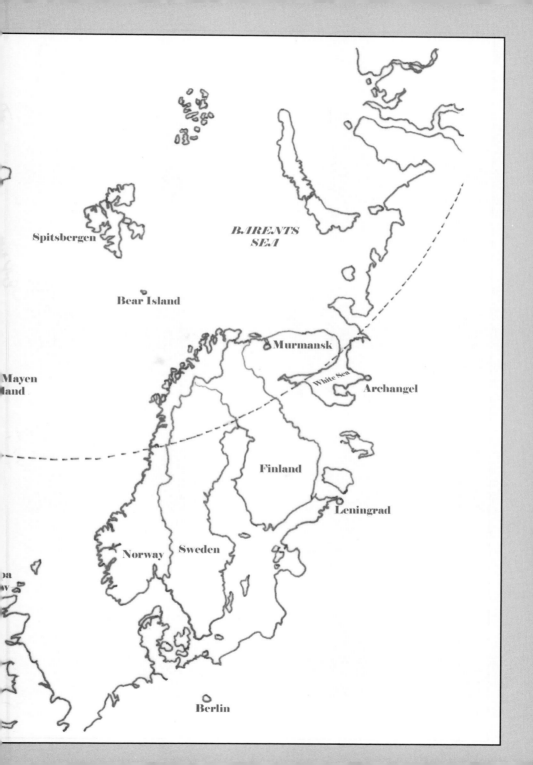

Philip James Ball

I was eighteen when I joined the Navy. Supply Branch (Logistics) Stores Assistant.

I was on HMS Victorious – she was newly built in 1940/41. We all boarded at Newcastle, then in May 1941 joined the Home Fleet at Scapa Flow. We went on exercises, and were then patrolling around the Arctic. We were on PQ15 and PQ17 – we joined with the whole fleet and escorted them to Murmansk. We were an aircraft carrier, giving cover if necessary on the periphery of the convoys.

We did see some go down.

Sometimes they were trying to train men as quickly as possible, to try and fill the complement.

We knew what was going on. We were a big ship. We could see the small ones being tossed to Kingdom Come. We rolled, but we could see much worse.

We went straight from Scapa Flow to Convoy Action Stations. We got the first convoy to Murmansk – it was mostly machinery. We didn't get ashore. We hoved off shore and waited to escort the convoy back. We escorted two big convoys in May and June 1942. The Russians were hard-pressed for weapons and all. PQ15 and PQ17.

The weather was atrocious – rough and cold – Churchill called it the journey to hell.

I was young, and nothing was going to happen to me. I suppose that's how we managed to overcome any setbacks.

The White Nights – it was like constant daytime.

We sailed and picked up the ships coming across from America, off Iceland.

We used to fill up with oil at Spitsbergen. You'd get shore leave to stretch your legs for a couple of hours – kick a ball around. I was so thin – I'd have my trousers rolled up my leg. I remember a quaint little white church in Spitsbergen.

There was no rationing on board ship. You had two choices: take it or leave it. We got the minimum of fresh produce, after the first week. But there was a fridge, so we always had fresh meat. Mostly it was tinned or powdered – potatoes, eggs…

We all had Action Stations. Mine was in the Ammunition Room – down at least nine or ten decks, with watertight doors. The first time was scary, but you got used to it. I didn't take any books down, but we played Ludo, or 'Uckers'. There were about twenty others there – including two Non-commissioned Officers and a Chief Petty Officer. In case the aircraft wanted ammunition.

When we hit very cold weather, you could feel the massive waves. The sea water froze. It could be very dangerous. You had to chip the ice off.

I've been out of the Navy longer than I was in it. I was thirty-five years in it.

When we were on our way back, we knew we were going to Scapa Flow, but when the convoys were delayed for a while because of bad weather, we the Victorious were pulled out and joined H Force escorting convoys to Malta.

The Italians attacked us. We were hit – a bomb ricocheted off the deck. We got back to Malta and then back to Britain.

In between the convoys we were part of the Home Fleet based at Scapa Flow. Shore leave would be granted for three or four hours, mainly for sport or walking. There would be thousands of men. Six or seven thousand men.

Scapa Flow was bleak.

There was always a friendly rivalry between ships – and very raucous matches. You shouted loudly for your team. I had played rugby at school, and I played hockey in the forces.

There were horrendous seas. It was pretty frightening. You could *not* go up on deck, though you could move around most of the ship. We used to feel very very sorry for the minesweepers and the frigates.

I can't think of the names. Back in Scapa Flow, we would invite a ship's company on board for a jar of tea and sticky buns.

There was a cinema – mostly musicals as far as I remember. And the ship held a concert party. Not then, but later on, at the Naval Air Station at Eglinton, there was a pantomime. Yes we were in drag.

We had our own churches on board – all denominations: Church of England; there was a Catholic Padre; the Free Churches – Baptist, Presbyterian, Congregational, Methodist. You could choose – when there was time for a Sunday Service.

On Parade, Roman Catholics were told to 'fall out'. Lots of men suddenly turned Roman Catholic (and went for a smoke).

You went to Corporal, then Petty Officer, then Chief Petty Officer. Then you would have had to take exams.

I wasn't called up initially – I had to pass an exam. I lived in Penzance in Cornwall and took the train to Devonport, Plymouth. There were a hundred men taking a written exam for entry into the Royal Navy. The war hadn't started. I liked figures and I passed. I wanted to go into Supplies. At the time I was working for an Estate Agent. My best friend was keen too, but he went into the Army.

You had to sign up for twelve years. I said, *Can't I sign up for longer?*

After twelve years we were in Peace. I was married in 1946 – I was in Hong Kong at the time. My twelve years was nearly up, but then the Korean War broke out and everyone had their time extended by  eighteen months. By then I was Chief Petty Officer, and I decided to stay on and make the Navy my career.

In 1955 I was Commissioned as an Officer. I came up through the ranks: Warrant Officer > Sub Lieutenant > Lieutenant > Lieutenant Commander > Commander.

The Victorious was withdrawn for Operation Pedestal supplying Malta, then reverted back to the convoys.

In November/December 1942, I was withdrawn from HMS Victorious and sent to Inveraray, where Special Forces were trained by Royal Marines. I was shifted to a destroyer. It was different from a carrier – smaller.

It was so strange. I was involved in convoys after Singapore fell – they still maintained a fleet, and I was on HMS Racehorse *escorting* the Victorious! And in 1948, as Petty Officer, I was sent to a training ship as part of the crew, and it turned out to be the Victorious.

I was sent to Hong Kong – we had a young daughter – the Korean War was on. My job was in the dockyard looking after the ships going to Korea and back again.

Philip's wife, Jackie: In December 1946 we were married. I got used to his absence. But as soon as he was outside the breakwater something happened – my daughter broke her leg, or the electrics went …
There were no Naval married quarters, the way there are in the Army. We had seventeen house moves.

Philip: When I received the British Arctic Medal, the Royal Naval Reserve in Belfast held a reception in HMS Hibernia – Thiepval Barracks in Lisburn – a buffet lunch. We were all presented with a pair of Hibernian cuff-links and got a tot of rum each.

One of my jobs was to look after the rum. There was a daily ration to those over eighteen years. If you were below Petty Officer, you got grog (one third rum, two thirds water). It was mixed with due ceremony in a big round tub – 'God Bless the King'. Each Mess would come in turn. It was issued just before lunch to each of the Mess decks – twenty or thirty of them.

I have two Russian medals – the Ushakov, and the D-Day equivalent.

> OBE
> 1939-45 Star
> Atlantic Star
> British Arctic Star
> African Star
> Burma and Pacific Clasp
> End of War Medal
> Long Service and Good Conduct

At sea we had nicknames – mine was Tiddly Ball (because I was smart).

On deck we had obstacle races, and we played deck hockey. We had teams for tug-o-war.

I have these photographs – there was a photographer – a Naval man on my deck. I suppose I asked him to get me prints.

I remember Trincomalee – Sri Lanka. Seeing swordfish and barracudas. I've seen whales and porpoises. It was always nice coming from the Arctic into the Mediterranean – blue sea, calm – it was like a revelation.

When the ice formed – it took incredible manpower to chip it off.

At Christmas on the Victorious the youngest boys would dress as Officers. They were sixteen or seventeen and they'd do the rounds – the inspections … they would dress up as Captain or Commander – the cap, the telescope, the lot … and they'd do the Captain's rounds.

King George came on board at Scapa Flow. Churchill came on board at Scapa Flow too.

———

Youth is a big protector.

Coming back – we'd have landed at Kirkwall and I caught the ferry to Thurso. I've taken a train all the way down to Penzance in Cornwall: John O'Groats to Penzance. We got as far as Crewe and there was bombing there. We had to stop in a siding – it took a day-and-a-half, the journey. It wasn't so bad when you were going home, you were excited – it was long when you were going back to Scapa Flow. The ship would have been having a re-fit and a clean-up, and one watch were all able to go on leave for about ten days.

Life on board was very communal. There'd be about fifty-nine others washing alongside you. In those days we slept in a hammock. Ours was a big Mess, and you'd be very very close together. You ate in it. You slept in it. That didn't worry us. It's very comfortable, a hammock. You were allowed to sling it at 7.30 / 8pm.

I would know a ship from its outline. Maybe not know its name, but I knew a County Class Cruiser, or … what type and class.

But when it went to Action Stations I was mostly down in the depths. We didn't see much of what was going on, but you could hear. We were escorts on the periphery of the convoy. If a small escort vessel was hunting a submarine, we could hear the thump of the depth charges.

Some of the torpedoes – you wouldn't get them in this room. They had to be lifted on by crane. And the shells for 6 inch and 4.5 inch guns … they're much bigger than you'd think.

I saw much more on HMS Racehorse – you got a ping on the radar, an ASDIC sounding, and we got close and chased. My Action Station there, I was with the Navigator on the bridge. Information would come from the ASDIC Operator, where the ping originated, and the Navigator would try and place it on his map… It seems a lifetime away.

We were rather lucky – on our Mess Deck there was an Able Seaman like myself, who belonged to the photographic section. We obtained photographs from him. Whether he was allowed I'm not sure.

The Cruel Sea by Monsarrat is about the journey on corvettes – much smaller than a frigate – it's well depicted.
On board the Racehorse we did several bombings. Burma and Andaman Isles, where we knew the Japanese would be. Several little ships went down. The Captain's orders were: *No Survivors!* So you could see the …

For people my age – who weren't married – it was a big adventure.

I've never seen an albatross. It's bad luck I believe, but I've seen whales, sharks, sea lions, porpoises, dolphins …

In the Arctic Convoys – it was bitterly cold up there. There'd be ice on the deck, snow on the deck. To clear the decks was the order of the day. It was important, because there would be extra weight on the ship. If feasible, without endangering anyone, a lot of the ship's company would be brought up on deck to clear the ice.
When in the convoys – either at Action Stations or on standby watches – I didn't get up on deck that much.
When we looked out and saw destroyers battling through, we got a sense of the extreme weather … it was shocking cold. What we went through was nothing like that.

I don't know that we were scared. I suppose – if you were on watch (four hours on, four hours off) – then came down to the Mess Deck, you'd think 'That's another watch – another …'

We drank cocoa – very strong. If you could cut it out with a knife, that was right. Sailors called it 'kai', a cup of 'kai'. It was made in the galleys. I brought it up to the point of watch. The Officers liked it as well when on the bridge.

I did pray. There was a little church on board, St. Christopher if I recall. We didn't have much time, but if it was possible to go to a service, I did.

I remember in Peacetime, the Royal Marine band, those tunes. I couldn't play myself – not even a triangle.

I love music – especially classical music. My father played in Penzance Town Silver Band. As did my uncle. And my uncle was an organist.

In those days, you had to pump up the organ. He would be down practising the hymns and he would need to power the organ. So I used to earn 6 d on a Saturday if I was in the mind to do so. I was about ten or eleven.

My best friend made the army his career. After the war I saw him once – he rose through the Royal Engineers to the rank of Major.
Places – I remember them.
I remember friends I had on board.

Nowadays I don't talk about it, no.

I do memorise it and the people I was close to then and what we did.

HMS Racehorse – South Asia Command – Lord Mountbatten came on board. He was a showman. We all gathered on the afterdeck, and he'd find an orange box and speak to us from the orange  box. A lot of senior Officers didn't like him very much. He was a man of his own mind and he would influence the men. He infuriated senior Officers but the sailors loved him.

The Home Fleet was based at Scapa Flow. We went out to join a convoy and over the tannoy – *The Captain will speak in three minutes' time.* We heard the sad sad news that the Hood had been sunk. It put a pall on the whole ship. It was a mighty ship. A huge toll. There were three survivors.

I had the privilege of meeting them in Northern Ireland. One was a Telegraphist – he lived next door. The Able Seaman I didn't meet, but the Midshipman lived at Eglinton too. We'd been living in married quarters for twelve months or more, and I didn't know until Jackie got talking to his wife. She said her husband was a famous fellow but doesn't talk about it. He said he was lucky. A shell went through the funnel and down into the ammunition room. He was in the water, struggling to get up – three of them – out of one thousand four hundred and eighteen men.

It frightened us. It made us think. I think we were on our way to pick up a convoy at Iceland.
It made us all think a bit. I suppose we all felt we were close to where it happened … Three men out of a whole ship's company …

Jackie: They found the Hood, and they had a service. They asked Teddy what would they do – he said *Leave them* … If there were any left …

Philip: One thousand four hundred and eighteen – like a whole village being lost.

The small ships – they would tie up alongside. We had to anchor way off. We didn't get to know the local population. The crew of the smaller ships did.

Jackie: Friends would say *How are you? Well when he comes home, you must come and have dinner,* and I'd think *Why can't I come now?*

William McBride

I was in the Merchant Navy.

Merchant ships went out of Belfast to all over, mostly Canada.
You went anywhere and picked it up and took it to anywhere.

It was always on my mind to join.
If it hadn't been merchant ships I would have joined the Royal anyway.

You just went and picked up stuff for somebody who wanted stuff.

The Convoys were very well protected – you felt safe.
They ended up that you were really converted into an armed ship as
well – we ended up protecting the convoys.
I happened to be on one of the ships that happened to be on the
outside.

I can't swim. Still can't. Never thought about it.

I was on different ships – mostly Headline Ships out of Belfast.
If they were signing on in Belfast you would have gone.
Tons of times – you would have went because your friends were going.

I've seen plenty of ships being sunk.
There would have been people I knew on board.

I don't know that I feel lucky.
It was my choosing.
It wasn't that I was forced to do it.

It really started at Gravesend Sea School.

I was a Bosun – or whatever came up.

There wasn't so much attacking the convoys from the air.

I never saw a U-boat.

We were able to get ashore in Russia.

Ach – you've memories all the time.

I really enjoyed it too –
It wasn't I was forced to do that.

I really liked the sea and the people on the ships who could bind
together.

Ruski danski eebat owera.

You were mixed up with that many.

I have drunk vodka and no matter what there was.

Paddy May Pariski?

I made friends with anybody – to tell you the truth …

In the Merchant Navy you could have got orders to go such and such a place and pick up more cargo … That was my life. There wasn't …

I don't dream about the sea or ice.

The only thing is – I remember we were on our way up to Russia and ice-breakers were escorting us in to the White Sea, and German bombers came over and they bombed the two ice-breakers and we were stuck up there until winter was over … because we couldn't get out … because they had bombed the two ice-breakers. Months – you were up there and you couldn't get out. The two ice-breakers – the German bombers put them out of action.

We had our own food.
You were glad of it.
No such thing as a ration of rum. If you had rum on you, it was yours
– you had brought it.

You couldn't say really much changed from war to peacetime.
There was always a gun on a merchant ship.
At the latter end of the war, I was on a ship and we had all kinds of
bombs, aircraft defence …
They had you more or less taken over by the Royal Navy by then. You
operated it all …

If they were attacking the convoy – you were always having a fear there
of …
There was gunners put on the ships.
You were trained to be a gunner yourself anyway.

You just got used to it being daylight all the time, or dark.

Whale? We had seen several of the fish.

Putin did the right thing, giving out medals. Britain didn't want us to
have anything to do with it. I never understood why that was.
I could never understand. You'd have thought they'd be delighted.

Somebody was looking after me.

When war ended – there wasn't the same excitement.

If the Headline boat came into Belfast, you paid off, and then re-signed
on again.

I have been through the Suez Canal.

I liked going to Canada.

I was very fond of Montreal.

I'd made friends with people in Montreal.

I was a deck boy and worked my way up to Able Seaman (AB) and Captain.

With me going to Gravesend Sea School I would have been picked moreso than somebody who hadn't.

William's sons: People had no money, no TVs, no cars. You walked everywhere and cycled.

Our father was born on the Shankill Road. There was one phone on the corner of Agnes Street.

His father (my grandfather) was in the Somme. He was gassed and ended up in Whiteabbey Sanatorium. Our father was four when his mother died. When he was sixteen, he joined the ships –

at least it was three meals a day and a bed.

It puts everything into perspective.

I wouldn't be here.

Marty McAughtry drowned on the Kenbane Head disaster – Sam McAughtry wrote about it. My father is the last living survivor. This is a picture of the Kenbane Head.

William: People say *What's your recipe?* – You have to be in the salt water for three days …

Sons: Swim – it wouldn't matter in the North Atlantic – sub-zero temperatures – no more than fifteen minutes.

Medals

1939-1945 Star
> *General Service*

Atlantic Star
> *Convoys America / UK*
> *Sunk 5/11/40 age 20 on Kenbane Head by German battleship*
> *Admiral Scheer*

Arctic Star
> *Convoys UK / Russia*
> *Stranded by ice in Archangel after Russian ice breakers were*
> *bombed*

Africa Star and Bar
> *Convoys to support troops (Desert Rats)*

Pacific Star
> *Supporting troops facing Japanese in Far East*

Italy Star
> *Support to troops in Anzio landings*

1939–1945 Medal
> *General Service*

Arctic Medal
> *Service on Russian Convoys*

And the Ushakov

———

That documentary [about PQ 17] was no good, to be honest. A load of rubbish.

I was up in the Arctic many times.

Many times. As a matter of fact, we were there and the German aircraft sunk the ice-breakers. After they had sunk we were left there in the ice. They just disappeared and we had to stay until the weather changed and the ice melted. We'd no maps.

After they had done that – I was surprised. They just sank the ice-breakers. They could have sunk us. They just left us. They knew we were there. We were a sitting target. Unbelievable that they didn't take the chance of sinking us.

They just left us there.

What could you do?

You just had to wait and see what would happen.

We were headed for Archangel – we had to stay until the season had changed.

In a convoy you might have known one or two ships' names – but I can't remember any particular one. I remember the Kenbane Head.

We just fiddled about. Mucked about and kept busy.
We were well fitted out against the cold.

The billet – you just accepted what was there.

You would have played cards, but that would be about all you would have played.

I was a deck boy and worked my way up.

I stayed a wee while – not very long – after the war.

You get acclimatised to the ship. It's very hard to come ashore and work ashore.

We had many good times – not all bad.

I couldn't really say what was best or what was worst.

It'd be as well not writing it – it mightn't be authentic.
Anything could be said.

I was born into the sea.
I wouldn't have stayed at sea if I hadn't liked it.

I'm not a great swimmer, but I never feared the sea. Never.
I was fortunate that way.

I remember the ship going through the ice – breaking.
Ice breaking through – sounds a bit like a window breaking.
I could never understand why, after they sunk the ice-breakers, they left us. They knew we couldn't make our way.

The foreparts of the ship were extra strengthened – fitted out with cement.
You were a bit of an ice-breaker yourself. All the ships going up through the Arctic – they fitted out their foreparts.

There are names for things – fo'c's'le head and all this here.

I met many different people. I remember a Jewish fella joined us. I had breakfast beside him, and I said *You're not going to eat that bacon, are you?* He said *You turn your back and I'll eat yours too!* Maxi Zakang I think he was called.

We didn't keep in touch – whenever I left the sea I didn't bother very much.
I used to go ashore – I mixed with people of all creeds.
It's amazing how you can do this – at home you …
You have to be honest, like.

No matter what port I was in, I went ashore and met the people and socialised myself with them.
And no harm ever came to me.
No harm ever came when I was ashore.
Montreal – I made friends there.
Whenever you leave it, it stops. That there.
Until you're back the next time.

Of course, you never knew if you're going to be back again or not.

You had to mix with them.
What were you going to do?
Walk around like a zombie?

All the White Sea – solid at parts.
They provided two ice-breakers for convoys into the White Sea.

Archangel was quite a nice place – very friendly people.
As a matter of fact – we made friends with people – Russians.
We'd have given them things. We would have taken sandwiches up with us.

It was a proper town. They weren't able …they were lucky if…
Even up there, so far up.
Suppose it was very difficult for them.
They were glad to make friends.
It wasn't all the people who would. I was told,
You'll be getting yourself into trouble.
I wasn't in cafes. Not in Russia. I've been in people's houses, but never in a café.

They had a kind of workforce – they were very hard on them, their own people.
We would have taken them up food and anything else – it wasn't easy – no – no way.
They used to be in big halls –
They were all living in that –
You'd have went up there and you'd have met the people.

I remember some of the boys on ship used to say – *You'll be ending up staying with the Russians.*
They had a hard time of it too.
I would have said that being warm to people kept me alive. I would have said so.

I remember travelling from the White Sea up to Archangel itself and it never cost me a penny.
It would cost thousands of pounds now to go on a cruise where I was.

I never got myself involved about Stalin or politics.
So long as they treated us well.

In the White Sea – they had a workforce. They were very hard on them. I complained:
Where I come from that's not allowed!
The boys on the ship said *If they get you ashore...*
We threw food over the side onto the ice for them. Leftovers. What we had finished with.
You'd have to be very hungry ...

I'm trying to think who was the skipper – an Islandmagee man – Freddie Milner...on the Kenbane Head.

They had a very hard time, the Russians.

I have a few phrases of Russian – some of them not very nice.
Ruski danski ibre dobre.
I have walked on the ice. You had to be very careful. You never knew where there'd be a crack there.

I don't think there was one on the ship had a camera.

The ship's company was from England – or a Welsh company.

You were either alongside the quay, or anchored out and they brought you ashore in a boat.

I've no memory of it dark the whole time or light the whole time.

On the Russian Convoys we had no Action Stations whatsoever.
We had one 4 inch gun on the rear of the ship for protection going into the sea.
We saw more action against the Germans in the Med.

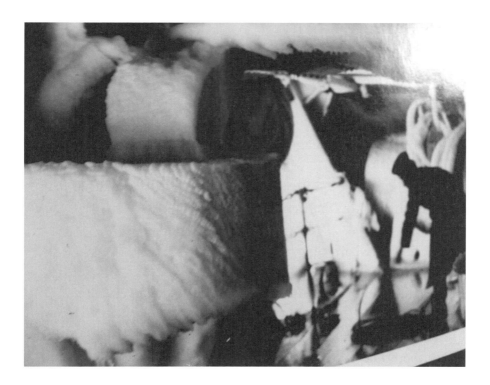

Then you'd come back and they'd be telling you
Don't shoot until you see the whites of their eyes.
That'd be stupid. I'll shoot when I fancy. You're mental. It'd be too late
then. You were dead. If you could see the whites of their eyes, they
could see the whites of yours…

On Action Stations I was a gunner on the head – up on the bridge.
You'd have been one or the other (right or left side) of the bridge.
Anti-aircraft.

We had very little training – *There's the gun. Use it or it'll use you.*

In the Med – planes would have come down below you – you couldn't
operate the gun against them when they were that low.
In the Med through to Port Said…They were – Italians were with the
Germans.
Some terrible things happened during the war.

To tell you the truth I accepted what was there – the food and that –
you could do nothing about it.
Some of the cooks were very good.
When I was deck boy, I was helping peel the spuds. That always got
me extras.
A method in my madness.

We had no uniform…just had our own warm clothes.
If you were an Officer on the bridge you had a uniform.

Most of the Skippers were from Islandmagee.

You joined a ship there. When you were going out – you passed
Islandmagee and they would 'toot toot' – to tell their people.

Flags and semaphore – I couldn't really say I could.
I could have done it with a lamp.
A Red ensign – that's Merchant.
A White ensign – that's Navy, Royal Navy.

I was married. To Emily.
I was lucky.
My wife's father was an ex-Naval man from the Shankill. He was very
'sea'.

I remember my wife wanted to smoke. Her father said *Emily's wanting
to smoke, Billy*.
He told her *Take a good big draw in…* She was as sick as a dog.
He had been a stoker in the Navy. He was over the age now.

I smoked because you were getting them cheap – it wasn't costing you.

Customs did search you.
So long as you didn't bring them off the ship.
They stopped me in Liverpool at the dock gates – *empty your bag*.
The majority of them were all right – they understood.

Whenever you have them on hand it's so easy.

I have packed in cigarettes altogether.

Cigarettes were costly, so they were a godsend. We weren't paying duty.

They were cheap on the ship.

I did drink alcohol, but not much – it was so easy to have – but I didn't
drink very much.
We had four-hour-long watches.
Whiskey – whatever you wanted – you were getting it cheaper.

The doctor onboard – it was just the Chief Steward –
You just had to wait until you got back to port if you were really hurt
or got sick. The Chief Steward would have done his best – he would
have had a course.
I'd no accidents or anything like that there.

You knew the world –
Norway
Sweden
Denmark
All those places.
The Norwegian fjords were lovely.
Some lovely places.
I went to the Norwegian fjords with my wife on a cruise.
Strange being on ship and not to do anything.

I've been places that even people who have been at sea a long time have
never been to…
I got ashore plenty of times.
I was a great one for mixing.
I didn't believe in staying on board –
I went ashore at night too, but you always came back to sleep.
Not out at anchor – but if you were tied up in dock.

Even out at anchor you were sometimes taken ashore on a boat.

My brother was in the Royal Navy and we met up in Scotland.
I hadn't seen him for a good while.
We were anchored at 'tail of the bank'.
I said *My brother's on that ship*. The Skipper got in touch about my
brother, and arranged a boat to bring me and we went ashore for a
wee drink.
It was nice. It would have been terrible if we hadn't been able – we
were so close – and anything would have happened to us.
He was called David – like my son.

It's a wonderful place, the sea.

You're out there in the ocean and nothing around you only the sea and
the sky.

We did have a cottage down in Millisle.
I wouldn't have known the names of seabirds – seagulls just.

I'm sorry I didn't take up something like this – I could have written
down the small things.
All the things.
You could have written a great book.
You just let that die out in your brain.
It's a waste.

I couldn't really say I ever met during my whole time at sea – I ever
met anyone I didn't like.
I couldn't say about anybody *I hate him*.

Indians … cooks … I couldn't say I didn't like anybody that went to sea.

Terrible – things in the world are getting worse.
They'd meet them in the street and murder them.
Troublemakers now – don't put them in prison. Put them on a ship.

ROBERT DAVID MCCULLOUGH

There were only fourteen of us got medals – way down at the docks.
It would take your breath away, all marble …

I was a sheet metal worker in the shipyards. When the War came on we
all wanted to join, but we weren't allowed because ship-building was a
reserved occupation. Ships were getting a hammering in the Atlantic by
the U-boats. That activity in the Atlantic changed their minds.

By the time we got there the war picture was dreadful. Them old tubs could only do fifteen knots – at most twenty. They were filled up with tanks and guns – old war material.

The recruitment office was in North Street – he had a doctor with him. I was the only one to join the Navy.

I love the sea. It's in my blood. My grandpa was a merchant man before the war.

I joined up and went to the depot in Devonport. There were two thousand men – all the hammocks hanging. We did training on a draft ship then went aboard HMS Ulysses. There were five of us ships – Ulysses, Ulster, Undine – U-Class Destroyers. They all had nicknames – HMS Useless, HMS Ulcer, and the Undaunted was HMS Unwanted.

There was a routine on the Arctic convoy. Part of the year it was daylight all the time, the rest of the year it was dark all the time. It would take you a while to get used to – it put you out of routine. We had big binoculars so we could see in the dark – red light.

I was a gunner – anti-aircraft fire. There was a stanchion on the bridge. It was like driving a car – you turned it like a steering wheel. A gun officer showed me: a plane doesn't turn right; it has to bank; when it banks its underbelly is exposed …

That pen'll be melting – you could get a job with the customs.

The convoy was about a mile round. Our job was to keep the boats in line, and depth charge the U-boats.
They had us in Norway first, meanwhile word came through that the Navy was getting a rapping in the Atlantic. The wee boats were very

exposed. They couldn't keep in convoy. The Germans had a long-range bomber plane. They caused havoc dropping bombs. There were U-boats around too.

We got back – I finished out in Japan – I was on shore when I heard the bombs had dropped on Nagasaki and Hiroshima. We were pulled back to England and demobbed from there.

On board – the canteen – the cigarettes – they had everything.
You could get Australian citizenship – they were offering it if you joined the Australian Navy. As soon as the war ended, they brought on board boxes of apples for us.

I was thinking of staying in Australia – they were offering good pay if you joined their Navy for three years, as well as citizenship, a job and somewhere to live. But my mother said *You've been away enough*. So that was it.

That ship – it was nearly all round the world – Indian Ocean and all. We'd been at D-Day and in the Pacific, with the American Navy, who wanted all the glory for themselves. Moving towards Japan there the sea was black with ships.

There can't be many of us left now.

Melbourne – I've never seen a place as clean in all my life. In Canberra they were building, and all of a sudden a curtain of dark came down … We went round into Sydney on our way back.

In Russia – the place … it had a swingy name – there was a big audience and all the girls ran out, and the men were around …

If the ships weren't unloaded you had to watch. A Russian guy gave orders and they took oil out of our ship, but the Americans put it back, because we needed it.

I don't know any Russian – just Vladimir Putin – right man – good now.

And Russian women pilots – Yow!

We went to Darwin and then round into Perth, then New South Wales. Melbourne is a gorgeous city. My granddaughter saved up and got a two-year visa. We all had to chip in.

You've cheered me up a bit – I was getting dull. I had a chest infection the other day, I couldn't see you.

Polyanna – that was the name of the place, or Ployarno.

The journey home from Australia was sad – I wanted to stay there. It would have been great – a nice home and a career. That's mothers for you – who'd have them.

We never saw ice – the helm just chopped through it.

In Ployarno they put on a show – they got a seaman up to dance – you have to kneel down and fold your arms, and he just keeled over on his ass – he couldn't make it. The Russians were very friendly and very thankful. The food on the ship was excellent. We got the best – eggs; bacon; steaks.

I've seen whales in the Pacific.
We actually lowered a boat with a machine gun to keep sharks away.

There was a deal that after the war you got your job back, but we didn't get a house for a year. I went down to the British Legion, and made a fuss. We've been in this house since then.

We were down there a few times. You had to wait to get into port to be safe – it was too far into Russia. They'd give us vodka. I drink bourbon.

Dream? No – they're nightmares. They're not dreams at all. They're bad.

There was nobody left when I got home – all the lads I knew and girls were all married. I went to a dance in the Plaza and I met my wife. They're all gone now – except one guy, Geordie McMoran – he's still around.

We had to go back to England to get demobbed. They gave us a nice grey suit, a trilby hat, two pairs of socks, a vest, two pairs of knickers. Somebody said to me *You look like Alan Ladd.*

I wasn't married when I joined up. It's too sad – you're only putting your sadness on somebody else – if you go, you go, and that's that.

Oh Irish music – 'Fine girl you are..' the Russians were into that. The Russians were very into you-know-what-I-mean.

Onboard ship you marched to church. They'd say Church of England on the left, Church of Turkey on the right. Those who went nowhere were off smoking.

———

That's a good secret: forty knots – nuclear subs can do.

We had to keep the convoy rounded up like chickens.
In Polyarno – there were twelve women in costumes. We were all sitting watching, and this man got up to join in the dance. He landed on his back. Nothing in between them and the floor.
In those times four or five convoys had already got up. They did a cross-attack – they were fifty to eighty feet deep, and we dropped depth charges. You could easy get shrapnel in the head. Or hypothermia. If you went too fast – with the twin engine – you could have turned round like a fifty pence piece.

I was a gunner – not a qualified one.

You had the Tirpitz and the Gneisenau – and over a hundred smaller pocket battleships, but well armed; but would have blew you off the water. Fourteen miles a shell could travel.

At Iceland, we hoved off – not allowed ashore. That's where, at night-time I saw a ship getting blown up. All the colours – then that was them men gone. You didn't hear it until twenty seconds or so. I never saw a thing went off like that in my life.

Then ashore in Japan, at the weekend we had things to do – we were going to watch the movie, when word came through about Okinawa.

They took us up to see it in the bus.

We were equipped for the Arctic. Kai – that was cocoa.
They gave us a tot of rum every day – more if it was your birthday.
There were 'sippers' who tested the strength.
Twins died once, on a frigate, of alcoholic poisoning. Better no relations on the same ship.

We had to do sea trials – care and maintenance party – welders wires etc. – you had to hang on with your eyebrows! – brilliant!

You weren't allowed to throw anything into the sea.

Robert David McCullough
Leading Seaman
Service Number
JX419348

My grandad was the last one to sail before me. The sea had me in thrall.

After the war, the ship was sold to the Turks. Church of Turkey …
I never thought anything about religion – I was too busy trying to stay alive. I had a good life. I really enjoyed it.

In the Pacific – I remember boxing – gin slings – darkies – savages knocking the pan out of each other.

Thousands of miles – hit? – Oh God Aye – you didn't hear the thud until twelve seconds.

Dorniers came over and strafed the ships from above, but when they got to us they had no fuel to get back.

Some other fellas once, they captured a motor boat, and tied it to the buoys used to mark – and lay in the heat. We came out of the mist *You'll get hung!* It was that dense – the mist in the heat … I can imagine the nose of our ship appearing, and them lying sunbathing.

I joined up with Gallagher from the Castlereagh Road. I was away out in Calcutta – there he was – there were three guys from home.
What are you doing here?
I thought you'd bought it!

The Ulysses had sonar – you heard the ping from a happy distance.

A ship is a community – you become friends. Somehow or other you don't follow that when you've left.

I remember – Mick – stand easy at 10 pm. I was sent down to get our tea from the urn. I went to the Galley and he wasn't here. He had a terrible turn in his eye. The skipper was going to put down a depth charge, and we found him – leaning into the depth charge drum … There were things that made you happy, but God love him, he just wanted to die. An awful thing that sickness.
I had it just the once and I'd done it.

Every night, there could be an attack. They could only do ten knots – you felt sorry for the merchant men. They had the hardest job – and the Russians as well, who were mostly on coal burners. You wouldn't need radar or sonar to catch them. You'd just need to follow the smoke.

Gerry Fitt was a stoker.

Ice – it cracks open – hard to describe – it cracks – an awful sound – echoed – echoed.

Those female Russian pilots – all good looking girls – good pilots. I don't know how many women … One would sit down beside you, wearing fur, you could nearly be sitting beside a bear.

They knew how to live, anyway. There was this big hangar – that was their digs – they had entertainment. There was a man with megaphones would give instruction.

It took two minutes for clothes to dry in the boiler room…We had dobbying – make-and-mend – darning toes in socks…

I didn't meet my wife until I came back home. When I came back to get demobbed, all the guys were married. I was left on my own. There was a dance in York Street – a big staircase – somebody called *Knock her out* – and these girls stole my sailor's hat and started throwing it from one to the other. That's how I met Bridget. She was tiny. There were a lot of us living in this house when the children were small. A neighbour's wee boy kicked his ball into the garden, and he came to door – *Is that wee woman with the big washing in? My ball's in her garden.*

They used to stop a boat in the Pacific, with a shark gun. People have their vicious side too – they'll get a laugh out of anything.

Spies took their lives in their hands. They never knew – a tap on the shoulder and they were gone. Gone away …

I've no photographs from back then – we had a fire. That's my sailor hat. You got your pay on that. You held it in front of you, and your pay was set on top.

RICHARD THEODORE CHARLES COCUP

I was a Lieutenant in the Royal Naval Volunteer Reserve.

I was Church of England.
My father was in the Royal Navy – Naval Chaplain.
And my uncle was Chaplain of the Fleet.

A bad early memory is being sent by my father to his parents in London, just for the experience of travelling.

I trained on HMS Ganges on the West Coast of England. I was in Cranleigh in Surrey, at public school. Two of us went out from school one day and joined the Navy – by signing some documents. They sent us to HMS Ganges where I joined up as Ordinary Seaman Naval. From Ordinary Seaman I rose to Lieutenant in the Wavy Navy.

I was on convoys up to Russia. Sometimes we were very close to Norway. It was mostly underwater anti-submarine work. German air action – it was more surveillance. You could see the German planes on the horizon watching.

On board I was Gunnery Officer and Confidential Books Officer.

I was ashore in Archangel. I was watching Russian men skiing, and one of them came up and loaned me his skis. I had skated before when I was at school.

Most of what I remember is in those two frames up there.

I have been in some pretty hazardous situations – where we were towing another ship and the tow broke.

I had the unpleasant experience of seeing my First Lieutenant on the way to Russia being washed over the side and washed back again. He was very lucky to be washed back again. Storms were severe.

Standing on the back of the bridge it was bitter. So cold – it was difficult to have a piddle. You had to turn away from the weather. And at night, rats used to get into my cabin – they slid down a pipe at the bottom of my bunk and would sleep at my feet – it was a warm place.

I don't think about them. I don't think about those times much now.

I have seen dolphins. I used to swim.

I don't dream about the sea.

I was on HMS Rodney – there's a book about that ship.

I'm ninety-two going on ninety-three. I drink gin, scotch, vodka.

There was a rum ration, but I didn't get it initially because I was under age. I witnessed the rum being issued. There were sippers, who tasted to see if it was the right strength for the sailors. Petty Officers got it full strength.

We got excellent food. Being an officer we had our own catering people and our own drink.
Only in port – I didn't drink at sea.

We had music from the radio in the Ward room, and an Officers' gramophone.
The only sport was when in port.

The rats used to run along the top of the railings. I had a revolver and used to shoot the damned things. We'd pick them off.

I had to row once, to be in charge of a boat taking a fellow officer onto a Merchant boat that had broken loose from a convoy.

And on another occasion two of us went on a boat to chase after a merchant man. When he came on board he had to stay with us until we reached England.

As Confidential Books Officer I had to record the signals. They had to be kept up-to-date. They changed once a week. It was a bit of a bore. Every time I came ashore I had to go to the Confidential Books Office to get the latest editions.

I got moved to Istanbul, Turkey at the end of the war.

When war ended I was in Italy for some time as an engineer with Ferrari in Turin – the racing car people. I like Italian food and good Italian wine.

I've lived in Ireland, and Northern Ireland for many years. Killinchy or here – and temporarily Dublin. I worked in Automatic Fire Protection – sprinklers, and retired twenty or thirty years ago.

I belong to the Lightship – I'm an Honorary Member. I enjoy going down to the ship here in Whiterock.

———

I joined up and was Ordinary Seaman Officer Class – I worked my way up.

We went on Arctic Convoys up to Murmansk on HMS Rodney.

I was Sub Lieutenant RNVR – signals and things like that. Confidential books.

I did not hoist flags or anything like that. A seaman did the signalling.

I certainly did not know the names of U-Boats or German Commanders.

I remember on one occasion going up the coast of Norway I wasn't particularly well. My memory's gone, of course. I was on HMS Rodney, and I was on the destroyer, HMS Inconstant.

The cold in the Arctic ... I remember it very well.

I'm trying to think. We used to trundle up to the Arctic. We usually –
I mean I would wear old sea-going clothes. I'd be up on the bridge
with my Captain.
A 4.5-inch gun? A bloody great gun. And the shells are massive. They
are, yes.

Of course we had radar – wireless telegraphy ...

As far as I remember, the Russians were particularly good to us. Glad
to see us.

Many times, of course, I've seen a ship sunk. I have seen people in the
water. We couldn't stop to pick them up. If we'd stopped to pick them

up we'd have been torpedoed ourselves.

In the Navy, surrendering wasn't really possible.

On one occasion I was sent away in a boat with a chap – a colleague, another Lieutenant – who was actually going to board a ship going to Russia – with his revolver – the crew were American – rather naughty.

I don't think my time in the Navy changed me very much.

There is nothing I actually miss – I was glad to get the whole thing over.

My earliest memory would be sitting on the front of our father's motorbike – nearly losing my balance. He of course was a Naval Chaplain, my father. He was away a lot. Of my family homes, Slawston is my biggest memory I suppose. I can't even remember the place I did my schooling – Cranleigh in Surrey. I didn't particularly like school, no I don't think I did. Ex Cultu Robur – the motto of my school – From Culture comes Strength.

I have a brother Brian who was Royal Navy Officer – about three years younger than me and I have a sister who's about ten years younger than me, I suppose.

I never wanted to be a chaplain like my father. I didn't have a very religious upbringing. Very irreligious, I would say. Seems to have brought me through.

I'm not really interested in tennis or football. I used to play rugby football once upon a time.

I'm not really interested in politics. I watch the things on TV – the politics there.

I attained very high rank. I was Officer class.

I never wrote poetry or kept a diary. It wasn't encouraged in the Navy.

Most of my working life was when I came to Ireland, I must admit.
My wife was from here.
I didn't find it strange coming from England. No culture shock.
In the old days we used to meet up on HMS Caroline on occasions.

I've still got the parrots – couldn't do without them.
I got the parrots when I first came here. I let them out this morning. Not outside – they certainly would go off. What are they called? Oh I can't remember. Please don't ask me. Please. One of them speaks.

I have donkeys, well – I give them temporary residence. They're nice animals – good stock.
I used to hunt here – horses, stag hounds – all around this area in the countryside. I probably wouldn't be allowed to now.

I was in Istanbul. What the hell was I doing there? In Constantinople?
… what the hell am I talking about?

I'm too old – that's the trouble. I'm ninety-three or ninety-four.

Regrets – oh I'm sure I have. I didn't just sail through life.

ISAAC HIGGINSON

Isaac: Aye – Russia. Look at all the flags on the side of the map. It's some distance …

Ach, I do. I remember my time at sea.

Isaac's son, Brian: He remembers, he told me, he got supplied with gear – duffel coat and all and from he left, it was never off. And you burnt it when you got back.

Isaac: It never was off us.

H.M.S. BLACK PRINCE

Brian: That's his ship – the Black Prince.

During his time in the Royal Navy he was in the sinking of the Laconia.

He joined before the war as a boy rating at HMS Ganges.

Isaac: It's away now

Brian: He was born 1918 – I have a list of the ships if I can find it.

Isaac: Too old. I'm ninety-eight. They say I'll hit a hundred. Oh I don't know.

Brian: That photograph is him in the Territorial Army – in Newtownards. The small one's his wedding.

Isaac: That was taken in Mulholland's in Belfast.
Yeah. Yeah.

Brian: You can see the white tapes – you wore white tapes when you were married, normally they were black.
And his stripe for four years' service.
And this indicates he was a gunner.
And this that he was a marksman.

Isaac: There were big 14 inch guns on the Valiant – a battleship.

Brian: He was a gunner with Prince Philip. Prince Philip was an Officer in the same gunnery as my father. Prince Philip met the Queen in Plymouth when he was on the Valiant. He and my father were in the same hockey team. They played other ships and the RAF – Prince Philip was centre forward, I think.

Isaac: Alexandria – oh we had some lovely times in Alec …
I've been at them all …

On the Arctic Convoys – heading up – the gun barrels used to freeze – you had to chip the ice off …

Brian: You wore gloves all the time. And even then …

My father said they went ashore in Murmansk and there were children –

Isaac: They took the chocolate, but the mothers wouldn't let them. [Shaking his finger in forbidding] – until they said they could take it, until they said they could eat it.
They got three or two meals in the shed across the way.

Brian: Aye – from them. The dockers etc. were fed by the ships – and they gave them clothes.

Isaac: I want to see that [pointing to what I was writing].

There's part of Russia and there's only four hours in the day, the remainder's dark.

Rum? We got rum every day – them that were eighteen or over – you had to be eighteen.

Ice? OH WHAT!

The clothes you wore – until you came back – then you destroyed them.

Could I swim?
Oh aye.
I'm surprised you asked me.
Some couldn't.
Oh Christ!

Dreams – oh aye, I have –
NO … No … no dreams – not going to …

A long way to Russia. A long ship's journey.
Murmansk we went to – Murmansk.
No chance. No. I know no Russian.

I was a gunner. A gunner at Action Stations, and when not, Director Layer –

Brian: He controlled the guns.

Isaac: We had one gun that over-ran itself and blew the other gun up. He lost part of his face [waving his hand across the left side of his own face to indicate the other man's drastic injuries]. He survived but [shaking his head] lost part of his face.

Brian: My father was at D-Day. On the Black Prince – he was on her for over ten years.

Isaac: You never know where you …
Where are you going to put this? A book? Oh I hope it doesn't get into the paper …

He's going away for a week – a week. I'm going to talk to myself.

I would still recognise what type a ship was from its outline.
Whether it was a battler or a destroyer. No battlers now. Aircraft carriers. They still have aircraft carriers.
I stayed in the Navy a good while. About six years.

Brian: Wait a minute is that right? – I was born in 1950, Noel was born in 1948 and John was born in 1947.

Isaac: Well I kept busy with your mother.

Brian: He came home, and my mother was working in Mossley Mill – my da got on his bike and went up to Mossley Mill, and the two of

them on their bikes went to get married. That was the best man in that photograph –

Isaac: He's dead now.

Brian: – and my Aunt Betty. They had a couple of days' honeymoon, then he left for the Mediterranean – on the Valiant.

Isaac: I was at the Battle of Matapan. We went on and destroyed the Italian Fleet. We were a battler. We were sent in. They never knew until they were hit.

Brian: The British had radar and the Italians didn't yet. It meant they could stand off and could shell from a distance.

Isaac: I was with the Valiant in Alec. It was a great port then.

Brian: Two Germans, or Italians – frogmen – on a mini sub – after the sub net opened –

Isaac: they came in behind the destroyer –

Brian: they planted limpet mines on the Valiant. They got the two Italians, they were prisoners, and they wanted to know from them when the mines were timed to go off. Admiral Cunningham asked, *Where have you put the prisoners?*
On the dock.
Well put them on board and ask them again.
They put them in one of the anchor chain lockers – he guarded one of them.

Isaac: There were eight killed aboard the Queen Elizabeth that time in Alex.

Brian: Nobody was killed on the Valiant.

Isaac: Oh you had plenty of superstitions and beliefs to keep you safe. Oh you had ... but ... you depended on ...

Brian: (interjecting) – each other –

Isaac: – yourself.

One time – the time she went – they had 4.5 inch guns on board the Valiant – five each side. He lost ... blew off (Isaac shaking his head and swiping his hand across side of his face).

Brian: Another time, remember, you forgot something and went back down the hatch and you were strafed and the bullets would have hit you, but they got him. He was your mate.

Isaac: He was. I do remember.

Brian: He was your mate.

Isaac: He was.

Brian: With the Laconia, the Captain of the U-Boat said if he hadn't got them, someone else would, because they were only going at eight knots to save fuel – not eighteen. Eighteen was all she could do. Subs can only do eight or nine knots.

And my da and his mates saved a wee boy of six or seven when they heard him crying. They went back and he was hanging onto the steps. They put him on a lifeboat. Then when my da was a POW in the camp in Casablanca – the men and the women were kept separate – but a minister came one Sunday and asked about a young fella who'd been saved and my father told him, and the next Sunday the woman and the wee boy came to thank them.

Isaac: I didn't keep in touch with anybody from those times – I can't remember. I worked in Doagh Mill and Textile Factory – I was the boss in it. And I was in the TA.

I never went back. I was only in Russia once.
Murmansk – it was nearly blown to bits.
They suffered – that port – terrible.

Brian: They got a terrible pelting.

Isaac: I was in a bar in Alex, and you know who was there at the same time as us? The Royal Ulster Rifles! I knew a fella from Doagh and met him. Wally – what? What was his name?
And I met him up in the barracks.

I was in Australia too.
And New Zealand.
I was everywhere.
Alex – oh Christ it was a good place. I know a family there. They lived there. We used to go. They had two boys and it was the first place I went when I got ashore, and I used to take them down to the beach…
Yes – they were British but they were out there. Och, it's so long ago now I can't remember.

Brian: No. For years he never spoke of it. Maybe in the last ten or fifteen years. We never knew the half of it. Mum died young.

Isaac: Your mother was only – sixty? What? Cancer. She had. That's what killed her.

I always – I could never get anybody like Isa.
And she had a mother. Ohh. (shaking his head and breathing in). She was (hard work) … she was. She had a mother, and a half sister, Betty McCrum.

Brian: Well your own mother – Lizzie, she married about …

Isaac: She was married four times.

Brian: My grandfather John – my da was three – he was a batman to a Colonel serving in the Punjab. He died of dysentery. He was only twenty-one.

Isaac: I was only two.
I never knew my father.

Brian: She married again. He was reared with his grandparents.
My grandfather John is on a memorial in a town away up in the Punjab – a spit from Afghanistan – in a war grave.

Isaac: He was buried when I was two years old. I never knew my father. My mother went to Canada for nine years – she married a man – two men – in Canada.
She was married four times, my mother. I didn't know them men at all.

I was brought up with my grandparents. I worked in offices in Stormont.

Brian: They weren't best pleased when he joined the Navy. They thought he had a future in the Civil Service. They weren't best pleased.

Isaac: If there's to be a launch of this, invite him too. He'll have to take me in the car.

Russia – oh I don't know anything about it. I was ninety-eight in March!
Oh yes. Everyone in the ship knew what was happening. What was happening up there, and what was happening.

Smoke? I always did. The Royal Navy got a cigarettes quota every month. How did you know? (I point at the packet of Mayfair Blue and the ashtray full of butts). They could have been his.
Him and Noel were in the Navy for...

Brian: (coming back in from another room) For 1 year, 3 days, 11 hours, 34 minutes, 15 seconds. We hated every minute of it. Another brother – John – loved it. He's in the Navy. Mother told us – you won't like it.

Isaac: [To Brian who is searching for a list of the ships his father served on, and getting out his medals] – What are you doing in there?
I didn't smoke before I went away. But I smoked when I came back. My granny twigged it. *You smoke!*

Aye, I said, *I smoke.*
I learned to smoke in the Navy. You could bring them. We were allowed so many cigarettes when we came home on leave.

I did miss it in a way.

I did the exam in the Queen's University for wanting to join the Civil Service. I did. I got that at Queen's University.

Och, I don't know. I was in the Civil Service for five? Two? Years. I can't remember …

Brian: War broke out in 1939. In 1937 when he was nineteen – you were only about three years in the Civil Service in Stormont.

Isaac: Then I joined up. There was a big fella there from Donegal – McConkey.

Brian: But you went on your own – you met up with him there.

Isaac: He joined up with me.

No – I never regretted it. No.

Brian: Then they fought to have it recognised. Tony Blair gave out an Arctic Pin. Originally Churchill didn't want it known – he wanted to keep it quiet.

Any ship sunk in WWI or WWII – if it's HMS (Royal Navy), it's probably protected as a war grave. There are rules protecting it. Merchant ships aren't as protected, that's why so many of them have been plundered. In the Titanic Centre, in the last gallery, there's a computer and a map of every registered shipwreck. In the Atlantic Ocean between New York and the UK, there are more wrecks on that trade route…

Isaac: (interrupting) Hey! More ships in the Atlantic!
One ship in the Royal Navy had 18-inch guns – the HMS Rodney –
the only British ship with 18-inch. The Rodney sank the Bismarck –
stood off her.

Brian: Them guns can fire two to three miles.

Isaac: You know, your mother was on the Rodney. The Rodney came
into Bangor and she went aboard.

Brian: I didn't know that.

There's a photograph of my father meeting Princess Anne at a
Buckingham Palace garden Party.

The Russians recognised the men and presented medals long before
Tony Blair and his wee lapel pin.

WILLIAM DESMOND PIELOU

Do you know the Isle of Man? There's a bay at the south and just above there there's a building that acted as a school where they sent us to learn radar operating. They spent a month teaching us.

I was born in Ballymena in Whiteside's Hotel. My grandfather owned Whiteside's and that's where I was born. I went to Ballymena Academy. I did my Senior Certs and things. As soon as I left I went down to Fleet Air.

Most of the time we were marching up and down with a crowd of others. They were teaching us how to march.

I was sent from the Isle of Man to Southern England. I got on board an aircraft carrier – American. It wasn't originally an aircraft carrier. It was a large ship used for carrying cargo around the world.

Nine foot in from the bow and the stern and they built nine foot high walls at each side – and they put a flight deck. They put steel ropes across the flight deck – ropes fastened down with springs. There was a wee path you could walk along around the outside – your head would be just above the deck – you could see.

When an aircraft landed, there was a hook at the stern – it caught on a rope. I saw an aircraft – when it landed and the hook caught and the

stern broke off. The chap was still in the cockpit, but there was nothing behind him. He was lucky.

A picture was taken of every aircraft that landed.

The other thing was – a small Navy ship was following us. If any aircraft fell into the sea, it was able to pick up the pilot. I never saw them doing that act.

We spent a year sailing the Atlantic. On HMS Premier I was Radar Operator, so my cabin was immediately under the flight deck. It meant I could step out and see every aircraft landing.

Before the Navy I tried to learn to fly – a Tiger Moth, a twin-wing. I was in the Midlands of England. I was fiddling around and I was told to go over to that aircraft and take it to that tanker and get filled up. I hadn't done any flying, so I lifted the tail – it was quite light – and I was able to walk the plane over to the petrol tank.

Another time, he was in the front seat and I was in the back. We took off. If you were sitting like this, you turned. You were level…You could fly upside down – a wee bit of petrol – flew past your head – I was with the instructor. When we landed there was this area of black tarmac with a railing and a big gate. One day the gates opened and out came a huge aircraft. There was only one made while we were there.

They decided I wasn't good enough to fly. I don't know why. They didn't tell me.

When I finished with the Tiger Moth I took to a single-winged fighter – this was in Canada. There were two seats. We took off and flew around. The chap never said a word.
When the war was over, they sent me to the South of England and I got a letter asking if I would mind going with the aircraft carrier to America, because it belonged to America.

In point, when the war finished – we went to Scotland. We still had all the aircraft on board. We spoke to the people in charge. Are we giving the planes back to America? – because they were also American. The Americans didn't want them and the English weren't interested in them. So it was decided when we reached the place where the sea was that deep – we would just throw them over the side. We built a wooden thing over – a walkway. We had all the aircraft on the flight deck. We actually had Marines with guns to prevent anyone taking anything out. We were going to America. They started pushing the aircraft over the side. Every single one of them was pushed over and sank. I thought that was terrible. They were open and sank quickly. Water filled the body of the thing.

In North Russia – we went ashore, and I was amazed – they actually had a shop up there. A young chap was standing talking. He was a Russian in the boys' training camp. He was able to speak English. I was amazed. The fellas with me wanted his cap badge – he was chatting away to us.

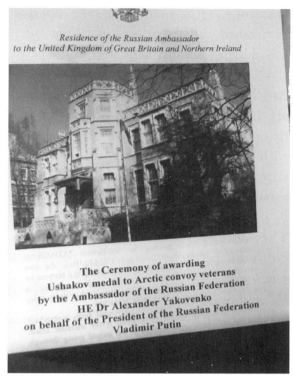

Residence of the Russian Ambassador to the United Kingdom of Great Britain and Northern Ireland

The Ceremony of awarding Ushakov medal to Arctic convoy veterans by the Ambassador of the Russian Federation HE Dr Alexander Yakovenko on behalf of the President of the Russian Federation Vladimir Putin

It was April – it wasn't dark at all, there was very little snow. There were a couple of people brushing it off the pavements. The pavements were just wooden boards.

This chap, he was in a yellow uniform, was talking to us, and suddenly two Russian soldiers, fully armed, surrounded him on both sides and marched him off.

There was an elderly man sweeping the pavements. He was able to speak English too. There were two huge posts and a cross bar, like goal posts and there were four ropes hanging down with loops in the bottom. I looked at it and mimed a noose round my neck. He said *No no.* He got the brush and hung it from the loops, and showed me it was for exercising on.

He went into the shop and asked me to go with him. He poured this stuff into my cupped hands, and wanted me to smell it...

Germany of course had taken part of Russia...

During WWII Germany took all of Norway. Norway had iron ore, and there were ships coming down the coast – ships of iron ore. The Germans wanted it. Our pilots would fly off into Norway. The Germans were in Norway watching out where their subs were, which were targeting ships coming from the US to North Norway.

We were lucky – we didn't get the Germans coming to us, but the wee ship following us around to pick up survivors, that ship was actually bombed up at the Arctic, and it sank. We lost those men...But we were never bombed. We had never met those men.

We were actually going past Scotland in the Arctic Convoy, and we could see a huge ship and the whole bow had a big hole in it. They had to zig-zag, and it had crashed into another ship, which sank. It was hard to do. That was an accident.

It was a surprise when they let us go ashore.

And recently we were presented with the Arctic Star. We got cufflinks.

We were made to learn to swim – in South England. They had a swimming-pool in the building in Portsmouth – they would throw a rubber brick to the bottom and we had to retrieve it. We all had to learn to swim.

I always loved going on holiday in the South of England – I was amazed how hot the water was. There were wee fish swimming round your feet. One day there was an elderly man sitting in the water, and he had a lump of bread and the fish were coming up and eating it.

I remember the one sound – when I went from the South of England to the Isle of Man I spent one night in London. I went up to where the fellas were already in their rooms. I said, *Have you seen these German aircraft?* We heard the noise of one – it sounded like a huge petrol tanker up in the air. We heard one coming over – there was the noise, then it went away, then suddenly it dropped down a huge explosion, and lots of smoke came up. I'm sure many people were killed.

When I was in the South of England I could hear these buzz bombs coming over all the time. I went to the next town and was speaking to someone and I asked about them and he said every day.

On board ship I didn't take the rum. I was teetotal and said I wasn't taking the rum. They said okay, and I got a penny a day.

I never smoked. Not at all.
I did stay teetotal. I've never taken it except I used to take the odd bit of wine.

After the war I was in the Reserves. My wife-to-be and I hadn't long met. I took her for dinner on HMS Caroline.

I did a science degree at QUB first of all. I was in the Dental School to get a tooth fixed, and I saw the instruments he used and decided I wanted to do dentistry. I went to Queen's again and spoke to the Professor, but my father had just died and I had no money. The Professor took a book off the shelf, and there was £8000 – a fund somebody had given the dental school. So I did dentistry. After I qualified I paid it back. I was a dentist and also worked in the hospital. My wife was a nurse.

A child arrived at hospital with a cleft palate and one of the Medical Officers sent for the Orthodentic Department Head, and he refused. I happened to be there and he sent me. That was the first child I saw who had a cleft palate. I began to get into that. I would see about twenty a year. I was friends with a chap who made dentures, and he had green coloured plastic and I got him to make a wee plate for the children, because it was soft and smooth. I had to take an imprint of each child's mouth – nobody else was doing that.

Anita, William's wife: It meant that the babies could be fed until they were big enough to have treatment for their cleft palate, which in those days was two-and-a-half years.

Desmond: We went to North Russia, and before that we went to South Norway. The Germans were there – they were actually contacting their submarines out in the Atlantic, and they could see them. The Arctic Convoys went down there. One of our aircraft attacked a German base in Southern Norway. I don't know how much damage was done. I heard one chap – a pilot – talking about a horse he'd seen, and chased it with the aircraft.

I never went ashore in Norway, but I went ashore in Russia…That's where we saw the chap in yellow uniform from the boys' training camp, and the Russian Army came and he got into trouble for talking to us. Two Russian soldiers marched him off.

I don't know any Russian.

We saw no women at all.

I haven't used my radar skills since.

But I did a lot of sailing. I was very lucky. My friend's father was a boat maker and we had a large boat for sailing. We sailed all round the Irish Sea and up to Scotland and around Ailsa Craig. A ship following behind us went close up to that hill and hit it. I was amazed it didn't go down.

My twin brother was a cartographer with the Royal Navy.

Austin his name was. He used to be in the Civil Service. He was very keen on it.
One of his jobs was re-aligning all the buoys – he visited some countries.
In South Africa he was out one day with a fella doing a flying exercise, and the aircraft turned over and he cracked his skull and broke his arm. He was the very clever one.

I made model aircraft – twelve model aircraft. I left three in the school. I don't know if they're still there.
He made that wooden carved cat licking its paw. I said to him – *A cat licks with the front of his tongue!*

When he died we got out all the things he'd made. The one I liked was a young girl on a horse jumping a hedge. We've a dog upstairs too.

This is our family crest – we were Huguenot and came to Dublin, then Ballymena.

I remember in Ballymena there were no cars – very few cars – lots of horses and carts. One day a huge crowd of people had gathered outside the hotel and there was a giant animal – it was an elephant – it had crapped outside Whiteside's Hotel. A man came along with a wide cart, and backed it up and he started digging into it. An elephant outside Whiteside's Hotel in Ballymena.

JOHN ROBERT CUMMING

In 1940 I was eighteen years old. I joined the Navy – I joined up for seven years and five on reserve. You do these silly things. I was back home and had been to a teacher training course, when I was called away to the Korean War. I was twelve months at sea again, then I resumed teacher training and started school teaching. With the 1947 Education Act all ordinary schools went to Public Elementary Schools – you had to go to school until you were fifteen.

For three years – we spent three years escorting convoys backwards and forwards to Canada and the US. After that we were on Russian convoys. Away up round the North of Russia. You have two jobs – one when it's quiet and one during Action Stations. My job was trying to fathom out the ASDIC pings – to follow a U-boat's course in the fond hope you'd be able to make connection with them and drop depth charges.

After the war I was in ex-servicemen's organisations. I joined the North Russia Club. I've been back to Murmansk and Archangel twice. Murmansk – and on to Polyarno. There was absolutely nothing there back then – only docks to unload. We were stuck there for a solid month. Our food ran out. It was twenty-four hours daylight.

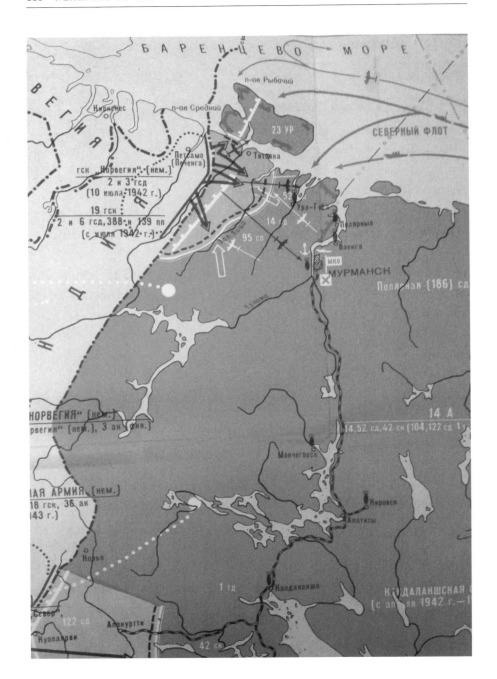

At 3 am the Russians arrived up with yak meat or something – some awful meat and some awful Russian bread…

God Russian's a desperate language. *Despedania kamba…*

Murmansk was only a wee fishing place before the war. There was nothing there.

Dervish – that was the code name for the first Arctic Convoy. It was to arrive in Archangel on 31st August 1941.

You had this plot here – and you listened for the ASDIC pings and plotted them on a chart and tried to work out the possible course. It was hit-and-miss.

In winter, the snow and ice and the nearness of ice – looking out at icebergs. And German aircraft flying over the convoys – oh dear – wreaking havoc…To that extent we were lucky – we weren't ever hit. I suppose you counted yourself lucky.

It was dodgy for the merchant ships.

A friend of mine – he was on the convoy that was given the order to scatter ….

Oh God aye, I could swim. I was glad I was able to before I joined, because the PE instructor insisted you had to learn whether you liked it or not.

I saw whales up in the Arctic. It depends where you are.

After we got back home, the next thing was D-Day. Then we ended up in the Far East, sweeping Japanese mines.

VJ Day was 15th August 1945.

We were out in the East – Australia – and there for the release of prisoners in Singapore. God Save Us. I can't forgive them. They, the Japanese, were cruel for the sake of being cruel. There was no need to behave the way they did.

It was tough going – tough – sometimes when things were bad – you want to forget them. You put them out of your mind.

But the Russian people suffered terribly…

When we returned in 1990 – Oh gosh – they followed you everywhere, big coats. Oh Gosh aye.
On our second trip back we were entertained in the British Embassy.

I suppose it was hard. Life was so cut-and-dried. You did this at a certain time…Like another world like. A lot of the teacher-training college students, they were nearly all ex-servicemen.

Och aye, I dream.
Sometimes it can get you.

In the Navy, following the Japanese, mine-sweeping – we were in some strange places – Borneo, Burma, Sumatra, Java, Indo-China.

I was in charge of supplies when not at Action Stations.
I'm ninety-four…You had a job when things were peaceful and another when there was action. It depended on the particular time.

At the beginning of the war this country wasn't ready. All these old escort vessels had been built for the 1914 war. We couldn't carry enough oil for fuel. You were always worried. The convoys would go up and down; in and out – because of fuel we always ended up in Iceland.
Eventually they took out one of the boilers and put in an oil tank.

The Merchant ships could do five or six or seven knots – you'd have thought at times you could have walked faster.

HMS Volunteer (rightly named, wasn't it?).

forty-eight old ships – V/W class. You'd have to go to Iceland or somewhere. You were restricted.

A rum ration – we did get that. The lower ranks got it diluted. The upper ranks got it neat. An eighth of a pint – a right good ration. Oh aye – it kept you warm.

On D-Day I was on an old Dutch Naval Cruiser – it ended up it was one of thirty old ships that were deliberately scuttled in a line – astern – to make a long line – a barrier. There was bad weather forecast and this was to give protection to the army for their tank landing.
We still had on board two ten-gallon casks of rum, so before we scuttled the ship, we lowered them over the side for the army. They went away fighting the Germans full of Navy rum!

———

The plot – the ASDIC folk here can pick up signals – and you'd be trying to track the course of the submarine, trying to see where it might be…There was a great big glass table, and a chart of that particular part of the ocean. You tried to track the U-boat course.

Look at that postcard of the statue in Murmansk – the Russians are very good at enormous. Look at the scale of the Murmansk statue.

That was the North Russia Club – in that photograph there's my friend from Comber, George Robinson, and another man from Bangor, Ashby Phoenix.
That is the British Embassy in Moscow – just across from the Kremlin – we were given lunch.

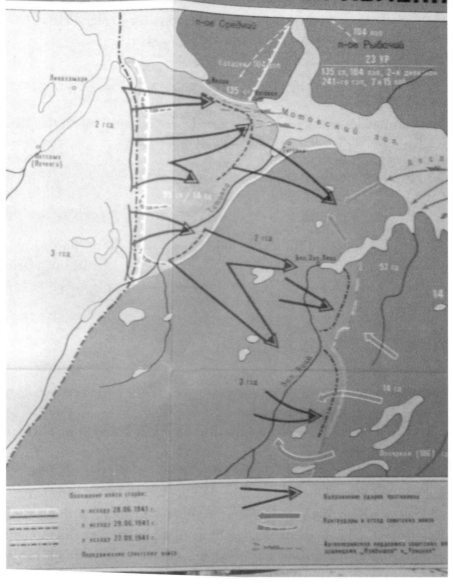

There's the Zadorniy ship. The sailors in uniform might look awfully young but they weren't any younger than ourselves back then.

In Murmansk there is a small British Military Cemetery 1918-1920. There's us marching in Murmansk to lay a wreath at it. That's the piper who came with us. Those were the days.

It's an awful language to learn, Russian. *Desbedanya* or something. That was goodbye, or something. I can't remember.

You got your rum from you were eighteen. None now – it's been stopped.

There's an interesting thing, too. The second man in this photograph was wee Bill Short. His ship went down and he was left floating about in the Arctic. When they got him out, a doctor somewhere in Murmansk had to take both his legs off.

In 1990 he was with us on that return trip. And in 2001 I was back there again. We were allocated a student for each group, they could speak English.

The Kursk tragedy – the submarine Kursk – there was a whole memorial room.

Back in the war we had a bad time. We arrived to take a convoy back and we were up there for over a month lying doing nothing. The Russians – God help them – had nothing to spare, but they still brought us a side of something, God knows what – reindeer or something. HMS Volunteer, being an old Modified V/W-Class destroyer, was built for the

1914-1918 war. There was no fridge on board. We operated from Liverpool and bread used to last for four or five days and then go off. We'd cut the blue mould off and carry on eating the rest of it.

Equipped? We were not. Look at that there snow – that's supposed to be summer time!

Leningrad – they had a nine-hundred-day siege. It started in September 1941 and went on until January 1944. They were surrounded by the German army. The bread ration was reduced to 35 grams of bread. Children and old people were evacuated across frozen fields. Half a million died of starvation, and half of them are in that big cemetery. They talk in numbers that defy imagination. There's this great big cemetery – a huge statue of Mother

HMS "VOLUNTEER"

Russia. They're not individual graves, they're huge mounds. They died like flies, God help them.

While we were in the Navy in the war we had very little information about what was happening. We wouldn't have known what was happening in Leningrad at all.
Normally – we didn't go right up to North Russia. We had three solid years in the North Atlantic with convoys from Liverpool to the coast of Canada.

Those old ships had to call in Iceland – they couldn't carry enough fuel for the whole journey. They could have if they'd gone in a straight line, but you didn't. You were always dipping in and out

On one return visit with the North Russia Club we saw fireworks in Lenin Square, Archangel.

With the convoys – we weren't anywhere near. They talk about going to Murmansk, but Murmansk was up an estuary and we unloaded as far from there – it would be like saying you were going to Belfast, but unloading at Carrickfergus. There were big cranes to unload. It was just a dockside. There was no point going ashore.
In any case, the Russians were funny at the beginning of the war. They weren't always that friendly. I think they suspected your better intentions.

I remember flying from Murmansk to Archangel with the North Russia Club. We had to cross over the tundra – mile upon mile upon mile – there mightn't be a soul living there. It's an enormous country – look at Moscow away down there on the map.

421 Class (Supply Branch) while in training at R.N. Barracks
Brostal, Rochester, Kent.

POST : CARD

28th April 1941.

CORRESPONDENCE   ADDRESS ONLY

TOP ROW							
1ST.	Chinnock	McConnell	Newland	Coombe	Jukes Kenney	Nilson	Best.
2ND	Penwell	Dyer	Detherick	O'Regan	Foster Cumming	Ball Birmingham	Ruby
3RD	Stuckson	Curran	Struthers Gray	P.O. BAILLIE McLean	Davis James	Coulling	
4TH. BOTTOM		Sedgemore	Houghton	Park Dawson			

L TO R →

There's a War Memorial and an eternal flame on the River Dvina in Archangel.

And I have these photographs of present-day Murmansk.

Old wooden buildings – they're still lived in.

The Communists did away with religion but they were beginning to build a new church in Murmansk when we went back.

The modern town is big concrete buildings – plain.

That's a big store, but there was nothing in it. The only things they had – they had damn all – were Russian hats and synthetic furs.

The Russians had women pilots – and women troops. Women played their part, oh God, aye.

I never told the children I taught. You didn't talk much about the war.

That's the Ushakov medal – that's supposed to be for bravery! In the Arctic. To give them their dues, the Russian Ambassador flew over to Belfast to present us.

The Legion of Honour – D-Day – that's what that's for. I was on board the Dutch HMS Sumatra. They were scuttled in shallow water – the upper deck was always above water…We were supposed to be off it, but the timing was a bit skewed. We weren't at any real risk – we just all went as high as we could on the upper deck.

I joined HMS Volunteer at Chatham.

I joined up with this boy – Millar McConnell (that was someone's surname and he got it as a Christian name). Och, he's dead now. From Ballyclare.

By co-incidence he had four daughters and I had four daughters. They say sailors don't have sons in case they're stupid enough to grow up and join the Navy. To guard against that possibility we have daughters.

That's Japanese money, used during the occupation of Malaya.

That fella in the photograph there – we were in the Atlantic and came in to Harland and Wolff in Belfast. I was able to come home, but that colleague who had signed up with me was out in digs. He ended up marrying the daughter of the house. I couldn't tell if he came back here to live – he probably wakened up one day and realised he'd married someone from Belfast.

Oh that photograph – Captain Luther – that was his name – he was inspecting something on shore, and he came skipping down the steps off the jetty and slid and broke his back. We never heard of him again.

When I was eighteen I joined up for seven years active and five years reserve. I'd come home and begun teaching at Gilnahirk, when I was called up again – much to the displeasure of my wife. Our daughter was just a baby. I was back in the Navy, on board a frigate, for eighteen months. I spent a total of twelve years at sea.
I was called up for Korea, but quite honestly I wasn't at Korea. I think they called us reserve lot up to man the Home Fleet, and then active servicemen were sent to the East.

You weren't allowed cameras – you weren't allowed to photograph things during the war.

Did you see that picture – those men – the picture of those men…in the water…

What terrified us most was the fear of storm.

William Joseph Growcott

I falsified my age. I was just seventeen.

I'm from London. I met my wife and moved here. I'm sixty-three years here.

I was sent to Derry, and joined an American frigate for the Western Approaches. That's an Atlantic Convoy word.

They'd paint the ship – a very light creamy green – for Russia. You knew where you were going then.

I was in the D-Day landings too.

I was in the gunnery – on a small ship you did anything – sometimes on depth charges.

After one month in Derry it was America. Tobermory, Scotland – two weeks practice. Then you met up with other ships half-way across the Atlantic – toing and froing all the time.

The trip to Russia took about three weeks – it was all about the weather – so cold and so wet.

In Murmansk we never got ashore.

After the war, we were in Spain. We brought four surrendered U-boats.

We just handed them over – nothing to do with us.

You didn't go straight – you zig-zagged.

I was just once to Russia – then we got ready for D-Day.

It was the merchant ships they were after.

We weren't equipped with clothing. We used to be soaking wet and freezing.

What you were frightened of more than anything was the weather – more than the Germans.
I have very distant memories of Russia – it was the weather but.

A fella – the boffer – the foreman – had been on the Mediterranean. He'd been burnt in action in the Med – Murphy – he had no skin on his hands or arms – he must have suffered in the cold.

We were there for hunting the submarines.

Everyone was in the same boat.

I don't see any glory in it. It was something you had to do. I don't see anything romantic about it whatsoever.

When anything happened, you had to get out of there. You never picked anyone out of the water. You had to get away.

You never knew.

We used to patrol off the Irish Coast – just off it – three miles. If U-boats were in trouble – they would get in there. The Irish helped anybody. You were allowed to stay a certain number of days before they interned you.

We all stuck together. If we went ashore anywhere – the same crowd hung together.

After the war was over, we didn't keep in touch. We were all glad to get out – to get away from it.

It's surprising how many people signed on. My father had been in the Navy before me.

The army, when in battle, they suffered. At least we could get washed – clean clothes.

If you got in the water, you froze to death…

———

You just wore old clothes onboard. You worked – whatever you got – whatever you had. You only wore uniform onshore.

I was seventeen. I wish I was still and know what I know now.

My training was at the Barracks School at Collingwood, just outside Portsmouth. Ten weeks – that was your training. Ordinary Seaman, then after a year or so, I became Able Seaman.

I was on an escort ship to a convoy – Atlantic into Ireland (The Western Approaches).

HMS Narborough – K578 the number was. You don't forget a number.

We only went the once to Russia – after that we were on D-Day.

The weather is the most atrocious thing – even today – the sea was so rough – you were always wet. Old duffel coats – when they got wet, you were wet – you never got them dry. Not the gear you have now…

The Merchant – they had it hard. They took the brunt of everything. We were bad enough, but they were worse. Survive – that's all they did.

Nobody says anything. You don't. You're sent there and you do it whether you like it or not. If you don't, you're in trouble. Everyone's the same. All in the same boat.

I still can't swim – no, and I couldn't. Funny enough, it wouldn't have done me any good. The water was a bit on the cold side. They used to give you – if you lasted ten minutes in the water – if you survived that, you were lucky.

I was in the 15th Escort Group – just months before D-Day. We had to paint the ship again back to normal. Going to Russia, it had to be light green. The crew had to paint the ship. You did it yourself, top to toe.
In terms of action, we had a bit of trouble, but it turned out to be nothing. There must have been that many wrecks. The ASDICs would pick up all that, and we dropped a few depth charges.

The tanker would be sitting there – they refuelled you and you went out again.

It was three weeks' journey. You never went straight – you zig-zagged – you could only go as fast as the slowest ship in the convoy. They were that short of ships, they used anything that floated. You had to put something up, you know.

The Russians wouldn't let us ashore. I was never ashore.

The supplies ran out – you always came back – the return journey – on corned beef and rice.

I was on a small escort ship – slightly smaller than a destroyer. She carried depth charges and guns of course. That was all. We'd be tossed around like a coin; like a cork in a bath.
We had to go on into the weather irrespective.

Ice – I've seen plenty of ice. I remember having a look at the mast – you couldn't have climbed it – it was thick with ice. Sometimes it was so bad, you had to chip the ice off or you would have gone down with the weight of it. The weather was worse than the Germans.

I never saw another ship being sunk.

If your luck was in, you were all right. If you weren't, you hadn't much chance of surviving if you ever got in the water.

We had a ration of rum – raw. People always kept it. A lot took it home – they didn't drink it there and then. You got it once a day. I never drank it. I tasted it once and it took my breath away. Do you more harm than good. You'd get a big lemonade bottle and fill it up. Most people at home were delighted to get it. It was very dark – like tea without milk in it.

D-Day was one of the worst for us. We convoyed the four big troopships. We were hit and it split the bows open. We had to head for home. We saw plenty of gunfire, but this was an accident. It was a floating harbour with four legs – they floated it across the channel, and it came into us. It was a job towing it. An awful job. It could have happened to anybody. It meant nothing to what was going on, but it meant something to us – to see this big thing coming at you.

I met my wife in London and we lived there for a while. There was nothing I really missed about being at sea.
When I moved here I never mixed up – kept to myself – nobody bothered me – everybody treated me well. Minding my own business I never had any trouble.
In the South – ordinary guys – ridiculous the trouble they were put to. It was desperate for the families.

We took some Germans, some U-boat men from Spain. Four U-boats up to Latvia to hand over to Russia. The Russians got everything – the

U-boats, the crew. Prisoners of War – the Russians didn't treat them well. They'd no mercy. We would have got the same treatment. Some prisoners tried to escape when they knew. It's bad enough, but when you knew what you were getting into – knew what you were going to…

Even in peacetime it's a bad journey.

I was lucky – I didn't have a family. Both my parents had died. Some of the guys would be listening to the news, about London being bombed. It was heart-rending for some of them. They got back and found they had no family at all.

The people making the decisions – if they'd been there it would have been a different matter. If they didn't see it, it didn't mean anything. These generals – putting fellas into battle, knowing bloody well they won't survive – it takes a certain type of person. Not everyone could do it. You have to live it yourself.

I don't think it could be expressed, what I feel. War is definitely very cruel. It benefits nobody, except the boys making money.

The nonsense that goes on here – it's a tragedy – they'd want to get out of here – they don't roam – they don't see anyone's side but their own. It's no good trying to tell them. It's like beating your head against a wall.

The memories stay with you. You don't say. Things that – in normal life – just wouldn't be.

If you could put down how people feel and what they see when they do these things…but you never could. You couldn't do it.

ARTHUR WILLIAM BEALES

That photograph is me when I was eighteen, when I joined the Navy.

That's my medal. I'm very proud. I think I'm the only one in Derry.

I have five sons – one of them is in Canada. I asked if he would come home – but he said *Dad would you go back to live in London?* I said *No, but I've nobody left there. Your brothers are here.* He phones every Saturday, just for a few minutes. I said, *You could live your own life here. Except for one thing.* I told him he'd have to go outside to smoke.

My youngest son is almost fifty.
Two of my sons get a lift up on a Wednesday evening, and we take a drink together and spend a bit of time.

I do all my own cooking.

In two months' time – September – I'll be ninety-two.

I've a lot of soreness – a very bad back. If I sit too long, I get stiff. I have to go outside and walk about.

A new woman moved in across the street and I could see her looking at me when I was standing on my step. I met her in Costcutters and introduced myself and welcomed her. I said *I hope you don't think I was watching you.* I explained about my back. She's very friendly – she sends over vegetable soup.

It's rotten weather. In May the weather was good. I was sitting out all the time.

They gave us a good do – the Russians – tea and buns and you could bring two of a family with you. I took my two sons up.

Even now to this present day my sons ask about my time in the Navy and the Convoys.

That's a picture of my ship – HMS Torrington.
It was an American frigate on lease and lend.
I was on it for nearly two years.
We'd escort – close escort – the convoy so far, and then we'd go into harbour – Narvik or Stavanger or Bergen, or Tromso, and then another ship would take over. We'd be in harbour for about a night and then we'd meet another convoy heading back.
We sometimes went to Tromso, and the Russians took over. We left them there.

There were four naval vessels in each convoy.

We had a Norwegian pilot to guide us into the fjords. We ran aground and sprang a bit of a leak, so we were sent up to Belfast to the dry dock, but the dock was packed. Then we were sent to Derry. The Yanks were still here. The dry dock was packed here too, so we tied up alongside just where Sainsburys café is.

I was here for about two months. I only knew my wife for one week and I asked her to marry me and she said yes. I'd been around the world and I'd been out with other women, but somehow with her it clicked.

I find people here very considerate. Both sides of the fence. I can't see what they're fighting each other for.

I worked in the building trade as a plasterer and painter.

We were working on a housing site in Limavady, painting prefabs. The woman came out and said *Do you want tea?* It was about 10am. My friend said we'd both like tea and she said *I'm not giving him none.* Because I was a Brit. My friend was furious, and she came round and she apologised.

Even here – during the Troubles – my wife got verbal abuse.
And my boys.
And I myself got abuse.
I said *Take no notice.*
Terrible abuse.
To give them their dues, most people came and apologised later on.

After the trouble died down, there was a knock on the door, and a woman up the road who had given my wife a terrible time, was standing there. And she said, *Can I come in?* and I said, *Certainly you can*, and she said *I'm here on my knees to ask forgiveness.* And she gave my wife a huge hug. She was grand after that. You couldn't have had a better neighbour.

My sons went to the College on Buncrana Road, St. Columb's. They all got good jobs – Dupont, Seagate and the Pensions Bureau.

I joined the Navy when I was eighteen years, on the 4th September 1942. I'd tried before it but I wasn't eighteen.

Between sixteen and eighteen years I was in the city of London working with my uncles as painter decorator. I saw more dead there than in the Navy. You'd go home from work and there'd be the sirens and you'd spend the night in an air-raid shelter, and you'd go to go to work the next morning and there'd just be a huge crater left. Whole street gone. I saw more dead and bomb craters and gas smelling and water coming out and no one to cope with it.

More bloodshed there.

You'd have to put cotton wool in your ears to stop the ack-ack of the guns, to sleep.

In the Navy once or twice we chased a U-boat or an E-boat. But I saw very little bloodshed.

When I was between sixteen and eighteen, my mother and two sisters were evacuated to Cornwall somewhere. I had one brother, but our own house had been bombed.

I was the oldest of the family, and they've all gone. They've all died.

Living over here with the fresh air, I've lived longer.

When my father died of cancer, he said to my wife, *You see if I was living over there, I'd have lived longer. I'm finished.* He died at fifty-six.

I smoked in the Navy. Fags were that cheap on board. Not even the equivalent of 5p. They were 4 pence.

I used to bring thirty ashore all the time. My wife smoked.

I only smoked about twenty fags a week.

She lived in Bishop Street, and before I'd leave I'd give her the rest of them. We'd go to the pictures and she'd nudge me and say, *Arthur have you any fags?*

I used to walk her home and the buses stopped at 11. I'd walk down Bishop Street and all the way through Yanks and Canadians and Irish, to where Sainsburys is now, to the ship. You couldn't do it now.

Every day you got a tot of rum when you came of age.

I send away to Portsmouth for it – Pusser's Naval Rum – from this magazine. It has no after effects.

You got 3d or a tot of rum each day.

Any other drink I get a terrible head.

In the Navy it's two on one – one rum and two water.

I drink one on one – I have a big eggcup as a measure.

Pusser's Royal Navy Rum – Steeped in Naval History

For more than three centuries, Pusser's Navy Rum brought cheer to British sailors the world over. First introduced for crews working in the tropics (where traditional English ale spoilt rapidly) in 1655, it soon became standard issue across the fleet. The daily ration of rum was controlled by the purser (or pusser) and only ceased in 1970 when the Navy decided alcohol should be made available on a normal social basis. Pusser's is a blend of aged pot-still Caribbean rums, with a unique and exceptionally smooth, rich flavour. At 54.5% abv, the strength is such that, if spilt on gunpowder, the powder will still ignite, hence the term 'Gunpowder Proof'. 70cl.

93751 Pusser's 'Gunpowder Proof' rum, £37.99

www.nauticalia.com

When my wife was living – I never drank it then. We'd go out more, and she'd say, *Why don't you have a bottle of wine and put your time in.* She smoked, but she never drank at all.

She used to chain smoke. I was surprised when she packed it in. *I'll believe it when I see it...* but she done it inside a week. It took me longer to get off them.

She was a great religious woman. She prayed to Padre Pio. She went over to Italy. I went a couple of times. She had a cure. People queued outside this house.

The Bishop knew about it and gave her permission. He got her a room in the Community Centre for one day a week. He said just one day a week – it must be very tiring.

I was very sceptical, but one time a woman came from Rosemount with a little boy who had an enlarged heart – you could see it pounding against his shirt. I had to go, usually, into the kitchen, but I sat on. He was going to Belfast for an operation at the end of the next week. My wife put her hand on. And then she said *He'll be all right now.*

Later – I had no outside light, and the doorbell went and a boy said is Betty in, could I see her. And he said *Do you remember me? I came from Rosemount.* When he got to Belfast for his pre-op they found nothing wrong and sent him home.

I had dreadful sciatica once down my leg. I was clinging to the mantelpiece. I could do nothing. The postman was limping and in a lot of pain. He asked if she could help, and I said, well I don't know, because I have bad sciatica myself and she can do nothing. But she saw him, and I heard the front door closing, and he was running down the steps and hopping into his van.
She couldn't help me with it – she couldn't help immediate family.
She was two years younger than me.

In Norway, we pulled in to a harbour, and another escort took over. It would be just before dinner, so we had dinner and then you could stay ashore until 8 am.
We went and got a lot of cheap drink.
People had no cigarettes, so we could get very cheap drink.
I paid for a haircut once with cigarettes.
I went in and said I just wanted a trim up – because when you join the

Navy, they just comb your hair forward and cut a straight line, then to the side and a straight line…I had black hair and wavy. I looked and all the prices were in krone, so I said *How much is this going to cost me?* He had a bit of bad English. *Have cigarettes on you? Two cigarettes. Two.*

We used to sit on the ship, and they used to travel around in row boats and try and sell us drink.
In Tromso it never got dark.
I was on jetty sentry once, you just had to march up and down.
I had this girl following me. We had a Norwegian pilot and he shouted down, *She fancies you.*
Ask her what her name is.
Joan – in your language. She thinks you're her brother. Her brother went away to join the Navy.
He had joined the army in Britain. *Tell her I'm not.*
She was only young herself.

I could write a book. I spent two years in the Battle of Britain. From eighteen to twenty-one I was in the Navy. I was in D-Day. I left there and escorted ships. Then I married and got out of the Navy and the Troubles started over here.

A woman came and interviewed me for *The Sentinel*. That's why I asked you if you were from a newspaper. And I was interviewed for radio about the war. A German girl. She was going to bring a tape recorder and record me, but she never did. *I would have been your enemy,* she said.
We were just doing a job.
We sunk three or four E-boats – motor speedboats. We torpedoed them. We fired so that the sky lit up and we could see them. We sunk three and the others scarpered. We picked up the survivors. There were

four men on each boat, and an Officer. Twelve men and three Officers. Our Officers took the Officers up to their quarters – they gave the order to *splice the mainbrace* and we gave the men cigarettes and rum. They were shivering and terrified. They couldn't speak English.

We sailed into Harwich on Christmas Day. The Officers came down to us then, and we had to stick tape over all their eyes. They were like sheep being led down the gang plank, being taken away for interrogation. That was the only thing. But when they were on board, they were just like us.

It was the same on D-Day. We escorted the Americans and the Canadians. We didn't know where we were going, until we were at least an hour at sea. They never told us in case somebody said.
We escorted them to two beaches in Normandy. The Canadians to Sword Beach. The Yanks to Omaha Beach.
The Yanks walked into it. They had no idea of warfare. We saw them being mowed down. The water was red in no time.

You got no sleep. They gave you tablets to keep you awake for two days without a break. They brought you food where you were. We went back and forth leaving off the wounded at Portsmouth.

By the time we were going to Norway, most of the places had been taken over by the British army.
In Bergen with my friend – we met two British Tommies. They were in a park having a smoke. We asked them where they were based. *That hotel.* We went up and a Tommy was behind the bar – *Charlie, give them a drink.* We had whisky. *Do you want to see our rooms?* They were in luxury – a huge big hotel room, and he opened the wardrobe and it was full of drink.
The Germans had occupied Norway, but we had chased them off by then.

When we were convoying, it was so cold. You couldn't touch anything outside without gloves. Every day you had to chip off the ice off the gun rack to keep it moving. If you got cold on your nose it turned into icicles. It's impossible to describe how it felt.

I used to go to Killybegs with my wife. We used to stop over in different places. And I worked in Dungloe for four weeks. Painting and decorating.

I can swim. I learned at school by accident. All the non-swimmers were at the shallow end and all the swimmers at the deep end. The teacher went out for a smoke – it was common in those days. I got out to go and speak to my mate at the deep end, and I was bending over and somebody pushed me in. I came up and kicked and tried to stay up. And after that I practised holding on to the bar. Inside a year I had learned, I had my quarter-mile and my life-saving.

We did life-saving with the girls' school. She pretended she was drowning and you had to hold her head. And if she struggled, you had to put your knee in their stomach – so somebody couldn't drag you down.

And when it was her turn to save me, she kneed me …I turned all colours…she said sorry later on.

There was a rubber brick. You had to swim down and keep your eyes open to get it.

I got certs for it and all.

In the Navy now everything has changed. Back then they wouldn't accept you with glasses.

My sons asked why we always wore wide bottom trousers. It was in case the ship sunk, they were easier to get off.

Jacket and trousers – thirty bob and one pound for the tailor to make the suit…blue collar, black ribbon…

I dream a lot now, but not about being at sea.
I've even started talking in my sleep.
I was in a hospital ward with three other men. When they brought round the breakfast the other men said, *You were in some fight last night. You were F-ing and Blinding all night.*

Now I talk in my sleep and it wakes me up when I get no answer. *What'd you do that for? What'd you do that for?* It wakes me up when I get no answer.

So far, it's just my back and tiredness.
I get up at 7am each morning.
At 7.30 I take my breakfast.
But when I sit down and watch TV I get tired.
I'm on six paracetamol but it only lasts about an hour. Codeines were just the same.

Twelve years or so ago I got a pain at the bottom of my spine. X-rays never showed up anything. I needed a scan, but the doctor came back the next day and said *I can't get you a scan. It'll be nine months. Unless you pay.*
I said *I'll pay* and it worked out very quick. The next afternoon I went to Ballykelly – a private place and saw a doctor there. In a day or two I got a call to say there's a bed up in Musgrave for you at 7.30 tonight. I said can it not wait, but no. I had to arrange for my wife to go into Gransha, and my sons packed and took me to Belfast. They put a tube down my spine for four weeks – I had a drip – I had an infection in my spine.

I'm going to the lady doctor on the 18th. She gives you rubs and sprays and a thing like a lady's corset.

I do my own cooking.
Twice a week a woman comes in, just for an hour, to help with ironing and cleaning.

I think being at sea changed me. I'm very considerate now, to anybody with pain. I can feel it myself.

A boy got his face bashed in by one of the guns. It was a practice run. It was his own fault. You wear pads and push the shell – it was a four inch shell – and it jammed and he came round the front and shook the gun to see why it had stuck – it went off and smashed all his face up – everybody was shouting at him to move. He survived, but…that was him out of the Navy.

I didn't mind the Navy at all but I wanted to come out.

The Arctic Convoy was the worst I suffered. The cold beat me…It's hard to describe.
It was all right below in the Mess deck. We were a Yankee ship, so we took in sea water to make drinking water. We had a fresh water fountain. It was the first time I was in bunks, not hammocks.

I was on a clipper for one week.

I had one of my eyes done for cataracts, and it's much worse. I can only see a blur now. I wouldn't go out at night time – I see too many shadows. The floor sometimes looks as if it's moving, like an earthquake.

I was a Coxswain – steering the boat. I had difficulty sometimes.
In Action Stations I was a gunner.
I was lucky. I was only seasick once, on the Queen Mary on our way out to America. They converted her, so a berth for two held six of us. Somebody had put a scarf over the top of the open door, and I remember seeing the wee blue light that was always on, and the scarf moving backwards and forwards, and the next thing I was in the toilet bringing up my stomach. That was the only time. After that I was fine. Others weren't so lucky.

We were in Bermuda – a luxury holiday place. We got green bananas. I'd never seen a banana. They were below deck and when we arrived in Newfoundland they'd turned yellow and we threw them to the children on the shore. They had never seen a banana and we had to peel them and eat them to show what to do.

Before we went ashore, we were lined up for inspection. The inspecting officer told us we were expected to behave with dignity…and that in this port there was a particular drink to avoid that would do us harm. He did the wrong thing – everyone was straight out looking for it. There were men crawling up the gangplank, reeling over the railings… As long as you could get yourself back on board and clock in and fall into your bunk…

We went from New York to Boston by train.
People would invite you out. You took a bit of paper and it had the name and address of the house where you could go for your dinner. They would host you. You tried to get into the smallest group, because they would send a car and take you to someone's home. There was always a girl for every man – and you'd be dancing to the gramophone – and then they'd take you back.

And the USO clubs – we were asked what sort of girls we wanted (blonde or brunette or dark) and we said we didn't mind. Me and my friend were sat at a table and two girls came out to keep us company for the evening. Nothing dirty, like, and you couldn't take them out – it was just for the night in the club. And a free mineral. The first one was free and then you paid after that.
The Yankee servicemen didn't like us and we didn't like them.
There were shows – famous people. Bing Crosby was supposed to come but he couldn't make it. He didn't show up.

WILLIAM MAHOOD

William: I think it was six weeks up, six weeks back – that's how I remember it anyway. Was it not?

Trondheim – Spitsbergen – we had to zig-zag.

I trained on HMS Rodney.

I was stationed in the South of England. They were very good to us. They couldn't do enough for us.

Oh aye – we went ashore – in Norway – they told us to get away hame. The Germans had moved in and the Americans had come to put them out.

Cold – oh yes – froze stiff, froze stiff, froze stiff – froze stiff – absolutely froze stiff.

William's son, Billy: I remember you telling me you got a roast potato or a baked potato and you kept it in your pocket to warm your hands.

William: Aye – I believe that.

Billy: I remember you saying the water didn't taste nice.

William: Yes – we distilled our own water onboard.

I was a Royal Naval man – HMS Black Prince; HMS Zebra …

When we got right to the top of Norway, there was a wee gillet – we had to sail all the way round there (showing me on the huge map of the world on his kitchen wall).

I was in the Merchant after the war.

I just handed up. I wasn't a gunner. I just carried them up, the shells. They were very very heavy. Somebody else fired them.

I was in Normandy on a landing ship – terrible – terrible.

In Norway they didn't want us anyway. The Americans had come to put the Germans out. They told us to get away back to England.

Giss nich nee – I'll come back and see you in the morning…

Billy: He has this German knife. He was supposed to arrest a German soldier, but the man had a knife, and closed himself in the hut. When my father eventually approached the hut, the German opened the door and said *British?*, wiping his backside. My father said, *No. Ireland.*

And the German put the knife in its sheath and handed it to him. My father would change his name to Liam and drop in the odd word of Gaelic, depending who he was talking to.

William: I was born 20th of the 12th, 1925, in Portavogie.

We had to zig-zag.

Billy: He has this here German flag he said he got from a motorboat. And the big flag – that was up on the Town Hall in Trondheim.

William: That's proof that I was there.

In Portavogie we couldn't speak good English. We shouldn't have dropped it. We were Irish. It was our language. We didn't learn it at school.

The Russian Ambassador? Does he want to meet me or do I want to meet him?

Billy: My mother used the knife for gardening. Wherever she finished, it was left stuck in the soil.

William: You coming here listening to a lock of tripe. Liam de Monhalt. Spitsbergen – Trondheim –
And LST 386…landing ship – tanks – did you get that?

I never smoked. I used to give my cigarettes to my father.

Billy: That was how he got the big flag down from the Trondheim Town Hall – he gave cigarettes to a Marine to get it for him.

William: DJX 568157, from memory – it mightn't be right.

HMS Zebra got damaged. It took much longer to get back. Waves split the deck. Sloaghan foot all day – 303 Enfield rifle – skin was blistered. We had to practise – one lot were British, one lot were Germans. You'd be running charging, running for others with your bayonet. Shocking training…By the time we got there running, they were shaking hands with us…

We lived beside the shipyard in Portavogie. Wee William Mahood was the boat builder – 'William Maghwood' they said. People thought I was named for him, but I think I was named for my uncle – he was William Mahood too, lived in North Belfast. It was a different family. I worked at the ship yard when I was very young. He'd send a boat out every six weeks. He'd put the keel down, then the stern and the ribs, then they took it away elsewhere and finished it. He probably sent me for the nails – I was a wee'un.

I left when I was seventeen and joined the Navy.
And I emigrated to Canada – to Verdun, Montreal – for five years, working in Timothy Eatons on 7th, I think. Well – 7th or 8th – it was a long time ago. It takes a good memory.

Tommy Maxwell – oh aye – he was well known.

I never was a Legionnaire I never walked. I wasnae in the Legion. I was too glad to get out.

I never drank – an oul blackmouth – Presbyterian. It was there free if we wanted it.

I brought the cigarettes home to my da. He was a smoker. He was a shoe-maker. He had seven or eight men making shoes under him – in Ballywalter. But they were teetotal and they didn't like it that he took a drink. There were six or seven pubs in Portaferry and it was his favourite port. I always liked Portaferry too. The ferry – that's the second strongest current – out straight through the lough. I used to row out to the light ship. I know the currents. And there was a wee island in Strangford Lough.

Swim? No. No – it wasn't any good to us. It wouldn't have been any good to us...

War? I don't know. There's been that much said half true and half untrue and not true...

I was on the boat. We didn't much get ashore. There was one time we weren't allowed ashore because we had grown beards.

Billy: That counted as 'improperly dressed'. You had to shave every day in the Navy.

William: A lock of oul tripe – shaving every day...

Billy: He has a Royal Navy clothes brush and a German stoneware tankard.

He went to Canada on that lottery-funded heroes' return. And they said he could go again ten years on. He wanted to but my mother wasn't fit. We suggested a cruise of the fjords instead. He wouldn't. No more ships, he said. No way.

On certain anniversaries the Russians send medals. Some of them are unopened. He never opened them.

William: Did they send them? The Russians? I'm glad you came. I didn't know I had them. I never wore medals to tell you the truth. I wasnae a medal man. Och I probably did know and forget them.

We chewed the rope, I know that – we were so hungry…

William Mahood
– his own written record

W Mahood – Memories 27.9.93
Devonport D.JX 568157

At 17 I joined HMS Black Prince in Belfast. It was a light cruiser. First Commission done one trip round Cloughy South Rock light ship trial 40 nts

Loaded with ammunition and torpedo trials in a Scottish Lough
Picked up convoy and went to Scapa Flow
Early next morning two watches called to scrub decks
Sailed same day about twelve
Picked up more ships on the way – all steam
Could only do about nine knots also had to stoke up at night only to avoid smoke giving away convoy position
Took six weeks to get to Arkangel in White Sea Russia
Allowed ashore
Supply ship brought out 10 tons of gold in wooden boxes about the size of bricks
Stowed in aft magazine
Brought assortment of ships back
6 more weeks
Went to Scapa Flow
Taken ashore to a dome to learn to shoot
Black Prince had a bakery so we got fresh bread and mugs of Pussers cay that is thick unsweetened chocolate it kept us alive.

None of us got any special clothing
We wore some of our own civilian clothing and a boiler suit
Sailed again and went in a dry dock in Birkenhead
Fitted with rocket launchers then sailed for Plymouth
Got a run ashore

Then sailed again to become the first ship to break through the English Channel
We went up and down the French coast to Brest close in
Told later they wanted us fired at so as to pinpoint gun positions
They didn't open fire

Black Prince had ASDIC and RADAR also JARO [GYRO?] on all
guns and spy glasses
If you picked anything up on your glasses you switched on and read
port or starboard degrees and elevation
Glasses and guns followed reading automatic
Black Prince had eight heavy guns 5.25 inches and thirty-two close-
range Oerlikons and Bofors and we could mount Lewis guns
Usually nothing would come near a warship
It was the cargo ones they wanted

Next night Black sailed again for Brest
We were close in and told we were being shadowed by radar
Near midnight the captain on bridge shouted Hard to Starboard
One torpedo slid right along portside then another
Five German Destroyers Narvik Class had Black Prince between them
and the coast
Got message back five Canadian destroyers coming to assist
About 30 minutes later Black Prince opened fire and star shelled
We had a new flashless cordite so they could not see the gun flashes
Canadian Destroyers attacked the Battle
Lasted about one and a half hours
Got message back return to Plymouth
Canadians claimed three enemy Destroyers sank
One lying on its side and one beached

Got ashore next morning in Plymouth
Then we sailed again for Belfast Lough
A lot of big American Warships were there and more kept coming
My father's uncle and his son were senior Captain on Coopers Tugs –
Robert John Mahood and Tom Mahood
I was at school with him

Robert John was in charge of towing the Mulberry Harbours
The water boat came alongside so I found out ... Sandy was the Captain
He had been in Waterford, S. Ireland, hospital having lost a few ribs and his leg 3 inches below his knee
We were away up above Holywood

A few days later on in the evening we started to leave in groups of fifteen to twenty warships
Got to Plymouth next morning and told anyone who wished to leave the ship to get on Liberty Ship for shore.
American Admiral on board hoisted colours Flag Ship (invasion?)

We sailed that night for D-Day
2 ½ hours at sea pretty rough strong wind and rain
Small landing craft sinking
Troops cold and very wet
Sea-sick
Had to turn back for Plymouth
Next night sailed again still force eight
Very cold raining
American troops in flat bottomed landing craft sitting on their hunkers fifteen to a side
Some sitting that way for two days awash

A mine sweeper went ahead of Black Prince laying white tapes each side with very dull lights at distances
D-Day again 5am mine sweeper swings to port along shore and Black Prince slides onto sand port bow to shore
5.40 am

Eight very heavy guns opened fire on Black Prince
I was on Port Oerlikon loading
Number second shell just fell close and covered us with oil
I wore ear phones so when close weapons on port side fired I passed
the order directly getting it from the gunnery officer
Black Prince was first ship to open fire 5.40am broad side of port bow
Firing was continuous till 11.50am
Guns very hot and blackened
Everybody shocked
Holding hands to ears
Got message from shore troops being sniped at from church

It would have been almost possible to walk over the planes each one
towing the gliders
All air craft painted black and white stripes
The sea was blocked with all sorts of ships
One bomber flew back between our masts

American paratroopers were falling away inland just like small clouds
Hundreds

The shore was blocked up
Craft sunk smashed
Troops still on shore after Landing Ship Tanks
The large tank carriers got their tanks and lorries ashore
German troops surrendering were packed on board and sent back
Not one German ship or aircraft appeared
They had no chance
After three weeks we returned to Newcastle

We brought all the empty brass shell cases back strapped to the rails
Black Prince fired five hundred rounds
Got paid off in Newcastle
Then given a train ticket to Dumbarton of Dennys Scotland
Boarded New Destroyer HMS Zebra my second new ship

Sailed to Scapa Flow
Picked up Convoy
Always went through Denmark Straits between Iceland and Greenland
The Zebra was a Destroyer smaller
Weather was so rough we could only roast potatoes and eggs in the oven
Held them in our pockets to warm fingers
Took very large convoy to Murmansk
Dropped depth charges constantly
Very scary
Seemed to be ripping bottom out of everyone
Everything froze up
Permanently dark
80ft waves
Zebra very often lying on its side
Many times funnel and masts level with water

Trip six weeks up
Russian small ships met us
Returned back with another convoy
Never saw land
Six weeks later picked up oil tanker a few hundred miles off Scapa Flow
Got some loaves potatoes

Picked up another convoy
Same routine six weeks up no land six weeks back
To tanker
Another convoy Murmansk again
6 weeks up
Broke off convoy with another Destroyer and sent up to Spitsbergen
near the Pole
Sea flat calm
Sailed up lough
Mountains each side
Early one morning two tall weather masts off port bow
About 8 huts nearby no life other
Destroyer fired one shot
10 minutes later small motor boat came out to surrender
Just Zebra and other Destroyer heading for Denmarks Straits
Four hundred miles off Iceland Gale jams wind guage at 100miles ph
Seas mountainous 90 ft
Zebra fell into trough
Living quarters flooded
Crew was stuck to deck head
Then fell and lying like jelly on deck
Zebra's rudder jammed
Hard struggle getting back to Iceland Rekjavik for repairs
Went to Viangar

Sailed again for Belfast
Got 3 hours ashore after 9 months at sea
NO food NO wash NO shave
No change of clothes
Nine months at sea without seeing land
Sailed again for Scapa Flow

Then to Norway to take surrender terms
Went ashore every port
Trondheim tied up behind 2 U boats
Boarded one got flag wrist compass leather suit
Went into Town Hall
Backout party of German troops marching round corner
Large tower on Trondheim Harbour
Only one Royal Marine on Harbour
Went to tower and brought back flag
Give it to me for 200 cigarettes
Sailed on to other ports to take surrender

Leon, Tingvoll, Sundalsora, Lofjord, Kristiansund, Surendalfjord,
Andalsnes, Stavangar, Bergen, Stenkjaer, Hysnes
Back to Belfast
Sailed again to Scapa
About 3 stone lighter
Tied up to buoy
Sailed next day for Plymouth
Coming through Little Minches terrible gale
Apprentice Officer on bridge
Zebra a broadside on
Waves came right over cutting life-boats in 3 hanging on Davids
Funnel bent
Gun turret bent to one side
Steel ladders ripped off
Everything on Zebra smashed outside and in
Pulled in to Scotland somewhere
Given train ticket to Devonport

To Devenport same clothes jerseys and beards unwashed

Out of train about Bristol
Naval Patron waiting 'Show your pay books'
Sentence
14 days stoppage of pay and leave for not being properly dressed in
white shirts and uniform
Reduced in Barracks to seven days
Extended at home to 21 days
Back to Devonport

Sent to pick up LST American Landing Ship for Tanks
Sailed for Greenock
About a week later sailed up some lough right onto sand
Returned to Plymouth on train
Spent night in tin hut no food no heat or blankets
Put in lorries next morning no breakfast
Then to more tin huts
Strip off all your clothes take them up to counter
Took chain and ID disc off neck
Given train ticket to Belfast
Any part of uniform you hand it back
Got pinstriped suit hat and shoes and a ticket back to Belfast.

27.9.93 W Mahood Memories

Civy Life

Went to Hull England
Joined ship City of London
Loaded barrels of herring
Sailed to Hamburg Germany
Walked over piles of rubble no property standing

Corner of building table four men drinking
Got up and left
I brought one of their beer mugs back

Second day in Hamburg saw Russian troops released all in duck that
is white canvass suits
Loaded pit props
Ship frozen to quay
Took heavy list
Still sailed to Leith
Went onto rooks Burnt Island
Put jumping ladders over bow
Could not get on to rooks
Slid off 3am owing to ebb tide
Towed into Leith
Ship was holed
Put up in hotel in Edinburgh for two weeks

Sailed for Finland Kokola and Xypla
Loaded pit props
Back to Scotland
Sent to London Wapping to a canal boat same company City of
Charleroy
Two trips awr to Brussels Belgium
Two bridges on way mast and funnel lowered
Stayed for a year

Pick up my third commission
New ship in Belfast Loch Avow Royal Mail line
Sailed to South Hampton then to Venezuela S America

Went to West Indies Curaco Island for oil
Through Panama Canal
For [four?] locks East Side
3 locks Pacific 2 Lange [Large?] Lakes in middle
10 miles across
took eight hours
Called San Francisco, Cristobal, Barron Quilla, San Jose, Wymington,
Los Angeles, Canada, Vancouver Island, New Westminster, Vancouver
City

Trip back by Panama to Southampton
Back home went to S. Ireland Waterford
Sailed on Torr Head for St. Johns Canada
Took train to Montreal

Lived in Verdun for 5 years Lasall Bvd
Was stock keeper on eighth floor 5 years for T. Eaton
Left
Sorry
Got train
Over eight hours to New York
Got room in Lexington Hotel
Moved to Second Street 50 yds from United Nations Building
Walked round Waldorf Astoria Bronx Park Zoo Broadway
Violet Yvonne and I went right to the top of the Empire State
Building
Then we all got on the Queen Mary and sailed for Southampton

Settled in NTards
Started wholesale fruit business
Bought 4 acres ground and built the third bungalo in NtArds
Should have stayed in Montreal

W Mahood

JOHN STEEN

I think I spent four years from the latter end of '43 to '47. Three of us left town here – we were members of the Naval cadets – and joined up.

I made my first Atlantic crossing at the age of sixteen.

In the Merchant Service your duties were more-or-less detailed. You never knew until you were three or four days out at sea, where you were going.

I was on four different ships.

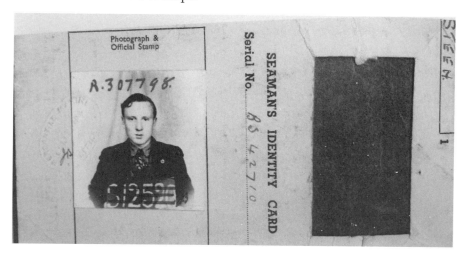

I was on a tanker to begin with.

I was very very conscious of the danger – because I couldn't swim, and I never left the cabin. That tanker was very comfortable and the food was very good. I was with that company – Eagle Star – for seven months. I was very fortunate. People used to complain about the food, but ours was exceptional – you couldn't ask for better. That was San Ambrosio.

You could be called anywhere, anytime – Arctic, North Atlantic …

Wherever the main convoys were, you could be detailed to go there. I only made one trip with a convoy into Arctic waters.

Unfortunately our time ashore was limited. Hence I changed to cargo vessels…you got to see a little.

I was not ashore at all in Russia or Norway. The nearest was Gdansk (Gdynia) in Poland. From memory I think the Russians were a few miles outside. It was early '45.

I had a camera. There were restraints on how far you could go with photography. I got to spend some time in Gdansk. I remember purchasing a complete dinner and tea service and a mantel clock for my mother. It's up in the attic.

And I purchased a camera for four and six English money.

That particular ship – I was the peggy looking after the Mess – you were able to

hold back sugar and tea and I was able to take it ashore and exchange it, along with cash.

That camera – my brother-in-law owned a pub in town – I eventually gave it to him.

One Christmas dinner my grandson asked a few questions and I started to talk (a rarity), telling him about the camera. The following year for my birthday they had searched and purchased an identical camera, converted into a table lamp.

It was okay taking photographs onboard ship – your ship mates etc. But I only got two full convoys, just as they were starting out.

Myself and shipmate relaxing on deck

Sometimes you were forty-eight hours at sea forming the convoys, before they all arrived.
It was an awful lot of effort getting the speed right. If you were slow you had to keep going…

I wasn't serving together with the men I signed up with, though I met two chaps – both deceased now. One was from Portstewart – Uel McLean – a lovely fella. He looked after me.

Another man – an engineer – a boilerman – by the name of Boyd. They were the only two I sailed with who were local.

It's funny, but they're the only two I really remember.

That's another chap in that photograph – we were on shore leave in Antwerp.

The Gneisenau – the Germans scuttled her to block incoming ships – in German-occupied Poland, near Gdynia – before the Russians actually took hold.

That photograph's another trip in those particular waters – that's coming home, myself on the left.

There was an old sailor on board the tanker. I can remember him – his name was Morrell. When this gentleman sat down to have a meal – I don't know what his complaint was – but sweat would have poured down both sides of his face. He made himself known when I came on board the ship – *Don't be worrying. I'll look after you.* If the bell went – the distress bell – he was always there first.

Those were all taken with that particular camera and we developed them on board. The lad in the Antwerp photograph was also interested, and he was able to develop them. I was just starting off. It was an interesting time in my life, and I enjoyed it.

I left in '47 and then I met my wife and we married in '49, and I came back to Coleraine.

I was connected to the family business – painting – but I was never happy with painting. I tried one or two other efforts.

Then the Troubles came, and I had to walk away from a very successful business. I just walked away. You either let it get you down or you walk away.

I have never said to my family about my time at sea until about a year back. My youngest brother came up and point blank asked me things that I never discussed at any time.

When I left home, I left a good home – I was spoiled. It made a man out of me. I witnessed things others wouldn't have known or seen had they been at home.

I was very lucky.
There were ships lost on two of the convoys I was on.
You knew nothing about that until it had happened. You saw Royal Navy vessels scooting up between, darting in and out.

My job was on deck – I finished up an Efficient Deck Hand. I sat the exams and became a Boatswain from Newcastle in England. I had discussed it with a Captain who saw my potential. The Geordies are lovely people to sail with.
A Star – three of the four vessels were armed. I was on the port gun.

The Harlequin gun fired so many rounds.
And there were 4 inch guns fore and aft.

On one occasion we had two Royal Navy personnel, and they would have looked after the guns.

Three of the four ships were Liberty Ships. They had been rebuilt. The record was four days to put one afloat.
It was a nice ship to sail on, but not reliable. It would have split in two. They were built in America (in two main ports) and in one place in Canada.

The San Ambrosio was a tanker.
The Samvannah was a lend-lease Liberty Ship.
The Ocean Stranger and
S. S. Asa Lothrop – she had a particular role, she carried landing craft as well as cargo. A very unstable ship – noted for losing even some of the craft. She ended her life in America carting timber, and there was

San Ambrosio

S. S. Samvannah Liberty Ship

Jack's Scrap Book

S/S Samvannah.   Jack Steen.E.D.H. R307798

The ship below was laid down as the Louis. A. Godey and completed as the S. S. Samvannah. Liberty ships as they were known as, had a width of 56 feet and a length of 441 feet, 5 cargo holds carrying 9100 tons of cargo. During my service on the ship she carried a deck cargo of tanks, jeeps and ammunition. Her armament consisted of one 3''bow gun, one 4''stern gun, two 37mm bow guns and six 20mm machine guns, crew were assigned a gun position on signing on. My gun position was a 20mm machine gun on the port side. Crew numbered 56 including officers and men. After her service the S.S. Samvannah was returned to the U.S. Government and scrapped in 1961. The Samvannah was built by South Eastern Shipbuilding Corporation Savannah Georgia USA. Hull no 1074.

loss of life through fire after she was handed over.

Many of those ships (with the exception of the tankers) were lease lend I think.

The landing craft were a long effort – square – a depth that would have covered the men, but stackable – they packed them in.

We weren't part of D-Day. We lay up in Scapa Flow and came down and were diverted to Belgium, and then shortly after, I can remember I was onboard the Ocean Stranger – up into Hamburg, where I witnessed children climbing the hawsers tying the ship to the dockside, to eat the slops out of the bins on board ship.

We would have gone out to everybody. We would go to the NAAFI – there was plenty for the troops – and we purchased stuff and gave it to them outside. It wasn't all sunshine for them either.

I never learned to swim.

In America twenty years ago, we got friendly with a Welsh couple (both deceased now) and he promised me that he would teach me to swim before I went back to Ireland, but the next day he collapsed by the pool and had to be rushed to hospital. We corresponded for years after that but I never found out what had happened to him…that put a finish to it.

I always had a great respect for the water.

I have a photograph of my uncle. He joined up (in WWI) at thirteen-and-a-half. He was killed on 30th or 31st October at the age of eighteen. He never lived life. My grandparents – when he was sent home wounded from the Dardanelles and the army discovered he was under-age, my grandfather – they were over-religious – *he's made*

his bed – sent him back and he never returned. My wife's father actually soldiered with him. Robert Paul (Bobby) 4432 – that was his number.

I never felt heroic, just excitement – three of us left here and another thirteen or fourteen joined the Royal Navy or army – just excitement – to see the world. It wasn't that you were doing anything brave. You never felt you had to.
Possibly our youth protected us.

Funny enough, there used to be chat among different crews, that quite a few skippers of ships hanged themselves for fear of the return journey. They were very courageous, caught in those convoys for years – they deserve to be remembered.

My effort was nothing.

When you were three days at sea, the skipper would inform you what your cargo was.

Prior to that, the majority of seamen would go down and look. There was deck cargo like tanks, army vehicles, 40-gallon oil drums, which were visible, lashed to the deck. Medical supplies etc. would be carried in the holds.

After three days – that's when you would be told where you were heading.
But it could have been changed at any moment. You'd be going to Hamburg, but end up in Gdansk. Where the shortage was, you were directed.

I don't dream about the sea, not a lot.
I never talked about it.
As a matter of fact my family are only starting to know me now. They're very supportive. I have three good boys, and a lovely family from them – nine grandchildren.

I was always coldrife. A grocer here used to say to me – John, wherever you are, use brown paper – inside the soles of your shoes and that. I felt the cold in my feet, in my hands, then when I returned home it didn't annoy me. But recently I cannot bear the cold. I feel it very much so.

The only thing that stands out as sound is – the bell going off – to get you to your post – if you were in the vicinity of the bell – it used to put everybody on end – make everybody very attentive.

I wouldn't recognise different ships. I'd be ignorant about that to be quite honest. Except corvettes, they would have scooted about among the others. And aircraft carriers – you couldn't mistake them.

You'd be four hours on, four hours off, watching for whatever was there – especially mines – well and submarines – which you never saw – sometimes late before you'd see or hear tell of them.

They weren't all bad times, the times on watches. Dolphins came up alongside and flying fish, believe it or not, coming up over the bow of the ship – that was enjoyable.

I would be of the opinion now that recognition was never given to the Merchant Service – even at Armistice Service, they are the last to be mentioned, if they're mentioned at all. And those men (especially those who gave their lives) deserve credit for what was done. The public are not aware of that.

When I came back, I did miss the sea, many a time, but I wasn't a good sailor.

Each ship had its own motion and you had to be on board for a day or two to get used to it.

I was seasick. One particular trip in the North Atlantic – the ship was on a degree of capsizing – she lost a lot of cargo – only three or four out of fifty-eight members of the crew were not sick.

The Boatswain was an animal. I remember being pulled out of bed – I was off-duty – to come up on deck. I don't think I was the only one who prayed he wouldn't see daylight. He was from Belfast. He had a son, we sailed with him, who was a gentleman.

I hope it's helpful.

D-Day – then they had all that in front of them.

A surprising number of dignitaries – Dr. Paisley's brother, Gerry Fitt …all merchant seamen.

The crew talked – we were always made aware, kept up to date.

My father was a singer. He sang for Glasgow Orpheus Choir by invitation. Unfortunately I could never sing. I have a grandson who went to Brighton University for Music. He's made his own recording studio – has artists come to him. It's what he has decided to do, and he's happy. But he won't sing.

Our family – way back fled Belgium from religious persecution – they were Presbyterian – then came here from Scotland. There's been a medic and a churchman in each generation.
We've always struggled and survived prejudice.
You'd wonder here, now – to hold a grievance so long.

Edwin Woodrow McCaw

Conversation with Edwin's son, Kenneth McCaw

I always say, when people ask me where I'm from, that I'm from the pick-and-mix in Woolworths. My aunt worked there, and she had a friend she worked with. She asked my father to come up when he was on leave, and she introduced him to her friend – that was to be my mother…

He was born on the 28th March, 1919 in Belfast – off Tiger's Bay. His father moved, during the Depression, to Mullingar, Athlone then Cork where he worked with the Ford Factory. They lived for eight years in Dean Street, beside St. Finbarre's Cathedral, and the school was right next door. I remember him saying *We could never mitch off.*

He had brothers and sisters. Irene, who is still alive at a hundred. Kenneth, then Edwin, then Desy and Sammy, who both died in their mid-seventies.

In 1935/36, my grandfather came back because of Shorts and Harland and Wolff. The family returned here. My grandfather was a Communist (and an atheist, despite being brought up Presbyterian). He abhorred Imperialism and it was to his great annoyance that Edwin decided to join the Royal Navy. There was a cold war between father and son.

My father said of joining up: *we were young and excited, we wanted to see the world, it was a job, and we didn't expect to be fighting a world war – to be fighting Hitler as teenagers…*

He was on HMS Inglefield and HMS Inconstant.

During the war he was involved in the Mediterranean, and involved in chasing the Bismarck, but the ship he was in couldn't keep up with HMS Hood. The Hood got in close to the Bismarck and was blown out of the water.

I know they went into Narvik fjord, and they were told before the mission to write letters home. They went up the fjord and blew up oil tankers. Messerschmitts dropped bombs but they found a fog bank and were able to hide.

He was involved in about twelve Arctic Convoys, I think some of them were taking food to Murmansk and Archangel. At that stage the Russians needed food more than bullets.

He was demobbed in 1945. He was called back for Korea, but he didn't have to go – he pulled strings and became Quarter Master in Eglinton, in charge of Naval Stores. He spent the Korean War as Quarter Master up there. I remember him telling me that on a Friday he would cycle to Bellareena (the nearest train station) – leave his bike unlocked; get the train into Belfast, then get the train back up on Monday or Tuesday, and the bike was still there, untouched.

There was a lack of proper clothing at sea. They had woollen gloves and long coats.
I remember him saying one of the first lessons was – don't pee outside, because it'll freeze right up.

He didn't speak. They didn't speak. They buried it.

A teenager – picking body parts out of the water…

Having survived the war they put it behind them – he was grateful that he was still alive.

One of the convoys – you'd have had merchant ships storing canned goods – they would take up their formation – even his own destroyer had to carry tins of corned beef. There was so much on board that the gun turret couldn't swivel 180 degrees – it could only stay straight. They actually used destroyers to carry the food. Fray Bentos probably.

After the war, he was a clerk in the Civil Service, and he went back into the Civil Service after Korea. He rose to Deputy Principal and retired at sixty.

Prior to the Ushakov, about seven or eight years ago – the start of the financial crisis – I came in and he was tutting at the TV, about the Greek financial crisis – the national debt etc. *That's my fault*, he said. *The European Union weren't expecting to be paying me my index-linked pension for over thirty years…*

THOMAS MAXWELL
1922–2011

Conversation with his son, Tony

All these things only came to light in the last fifteen to twenty years.

My father was a Marine Commando.

He was on HMS Cairo. There are differing versions. The War office

mentioned that he may have been in the Arctic Circle taking British delegates to Russia – or bringing Russian diplomats back from Britain. There were rumours that he was bodyguard for Mountbatten at one point – and my father mentioned that they were taking gold....

He joined in 1938 at the age of sixteen years. When the war was over, he was off the record for seven months. He was picked up and placed in a Mental Hospital in Bristol, and my granny had to fetch him back from there.

He was part of the Sea Service Battery –
Royal Marines 62.

He died in 2011.

He barely spoke of it, but sometimes you'd hear him, in his sleep –
Youse made me do it. I didn't want to do it – speaking in his dream.
He was probably shell-shocked. He killed his first person when he was
eighteen years old.

Twenty-three were killed on the Cairo in Malta.

He was involved with Canadian and American Marines. He got several
medals, including the Palestine Medal. I wrote and was permitted to

receive the Ushakov Medal posthumously for
him.

Even in the late 70s he would go on a bender.

He'd walk the streets for weeks and weeks and weeks.

He never went to the British Legion. He went once drunk and shouted
at them – *There's not one of them fit to tie my laces. None of them were
there.*

His brother Charlie Maxwell died during the war – he's on the War
Memorial.

I wore my father's medals once to the Remembrance Service, but there
are ones claiming continuity with the War – as if it's the same struggle.
They have nothing to do with the war my father fought.

My granny died when she was eighty-four, but my granda died when I was two. He had a WWI Medal. My granny – and my mother – should have been entitled to money – to compensation, or a pension for my father, but they wouldn't give it to us in retrospect. They did give it to him when we eventually applied, but they said she would need to have asked for it. How could she ask for something she didn't know existed?

It came back to him – we'd have to lie listening for his bedroom door opening.

He'd have drunk with the Pope. He made no difference. He did go up to see the priest a few times to talk.

He couldn't speak for the last ten or fifteen years.

ROBERT MCNAIR
1924–2014

Conversation with Robert McNair's son, Robert

My brother recorded conversations with our father, and it was extraordinary because though he couldn't, latterly, remember what he'd had for his breakfast, he could remember his time at sea.

His younger brother James was lost at sea on HMS Mourne. We have James' photograph album which he must have left at home after shore leave.

I remember my father saying of the Arctic Convoys that your breath was so visible, it sort of sank.
My dad was a particularly good sportsman. He boxed and played football for the Navy.

He would have sung: *The Old Bog Road:*

> My feet are here on Broadway
> this blessed harvest morn
> But Oh the ache that's in them
> for the spot where I was born
> My weary hands are blistered
> from work in cold and heat
> and Oh to swing a scythe today
> through fields of Irish wheat
> Had I the chance to wander back
> or own a king's abode
> 'tis soon I'd see the hawthorn tree
> by the Old Bog Road

Robert McNair in recorded interview with his son Victor, in 2003

Everybody was trying to get away into the services then. I had to get written consent from my father. He and his brother had had a good time in the army – and they had a trade. My father was a riveter and uncle Robert a boiler maker. But what was in front of me? I would have been a message boy. My mother and father had no objection to me joining the Navy.

I trained in the Boy Navy, mostly on the Isle of Man, where we were based in Cunninghams Holiday Camp – there were no holiday makers because of the war.

I joined HMS Victorious on 17th March 1941 with a crowd of others all joining the Victorious. I came with thirty or forty boys, all under-age: seventeen or sixteen-and-a-half. We were sent to the Victorious

No. 26   Series of 32

HMS 1902-1962

H.M.S. VICTORIOUS
Aircraft-Carrier
Launched in 1939 as a 22,600 ton carrier and performed distinguished service in the Second World War, the *Victorious* was completely re-built between 1950 and 1958 above the hangar deck and her structure fundamentally changed, bringing her standard displacement up to 30,500 tons. Fitted with all the British-developed aids to naval flying, including fully angled flight deck, steam catapults, mirror deck-landing aid, and Type 984 aircraft-direction radar. Now one of the Navy's most modern carriers, her 775-foot long flight deck can take all the latest Fleet Air Arm aircraft such as the Sea Vixen, Scimitar and Buccaneer.

LYONS TEA
Teacard albums are obtainable from your grocer price 6d.
J. Lyons & Co. Ltd., Cadby Hall
London W.14. Printed in England

– we had our own Mess deck. There was a Petty Officer and a Chief Petty Officer – they nurse-maided, or looked after us.

On the Victorious it was train, train, train. You had to train on a particular ship as a Boy Seaman. Also on the gunnery end – I was a gunner, the only one put on the Oerlikon – 20mm. The drum held sixty rounds. I fired when I was told to.

I progressed to Ordinary Seaman when I was eighteen. Conscripts were coming in at that particular time, trained in ten weeks. But when I became Ordinary Seaman I had already had two  years at seamanship. So I could have been put in charge of a man twenty-five or thirty years old – older than my father even – because he had only had ten weeks' training.

Quite a bit of our training was in harbour, because we had never been to sea. Then we went to sea. Initially we were in the Home Fleet stationed at Scapa Flow. A lot of convoys were going to Russia at that time – I don't know which ships were coming in, which ships going out. There were quite a lot of ships about.

Scapa Flow was a massive natural harbour. Most of the ships dropped anchor. Anywhere else – like Belfast – you'd be talking about tying up to a jetty.

We joined the Home Fleet – about October 1941. Then we were straight into a Russian Convoy. We were just part of a fleet escorting maybe fourteen merchant ships. The funny thing is, we got as far as Murmansk or Archangel and we weren't allowed into Russia. I don't know why. I was never in my life ashore in Russia. We took a ship of empty back.

It was ongoing – thousands and thousands of tons of supplies to Russia. The Americans brought it to us.

Oh yes yes we were attacked by German aircraft. Big two-engine jobs – Ju88s. They had the range. They came out from somewhere out over the North Atlantic and chased us. And the U-boats too. The convoys to Russia had to contend with aircraft as well as U-boats.
Mainly they attacked the merchant ships.

We had some ships sunk – The Eagle, an aircraft carrier. It was sunk because they could have put fighters up. What I knew about aircraft was nil. I was a seaman and a gunner. Ropes and anchors and things. We'd be strafed with machine guns. You were ducking and trying to hit them at the same time.

Did I ever hit any? Good question. If you hit them you'd have seen them going down. But I can't remember us ever hitting them and they never hit the ship. No. Yes. There was once – a different time – going to Malta. It left a dent on the flight deck – it marked it.

The Victorious was never on its own. It always had some escorts with it. Looking back, I suppose they thought we were valuable, so we were protected by destroyers.

We had seen ships torpedoed – sunk – quite a few merchant ships – torpedoed – in escort groups. To be quite honest I'm glad to be alive. If one of our frigates or our destroyers went – I was glad it was them and not me. It's selfish, but…

Cold. Very cold. We had only uniforms. You'd be trying to wear two pairs of trousers. The Navy always gave you a good overcoat. Fellas on the upper deck of an aircraft carrier with anti-aircraft guns – no matter how you go about it – you're out in open air. I'd be in ordinary uniform, but two or three pairs of socks. I found out then that if your feet sweated, you got cold. You learned to use what you could. In 1942 they started supplying us with duffel coats. It had a hood and toggles. And gloves. A Navy cap was no good in the cold – you'd have used the hood of the duffel coat. But your feet were always cold.

The sea was always rough. I think I was seasick. There was three weeks when we went to sea on the Victorious – a wave would have lifted the ship then *hit* you down. Your neck jolted. It was very sore on your neck. But when I'd been on the ship for two years I could have gone anywhere.

There was no shame in being seasick. You did bring your dinner up, but you kept going. Your mind was probably on your job – and you were never on your job on your own.

In the gunnery they have measurements for range and bearing and elevation of the aircraft and they would have passed it all on to the gun, and the gunner would have brought the gun round to the direction wanted. The ammunition suppliers brought the ammunition up from the bowels of the ships. They handed it up. All gunners are co-dependent on other people.

We had a chip and hammer for the ice. We chipped the ice off the turrets. We chipped the ice off the flight deck. I'm trying to think. Would salt water freeze? Would salt spray freeze? When the ship went into frozen spray – we got wise to ourselves and wore balaclavas. You kept it up so your face was covered and your own breath was keeping your face warm.

I don't know how many convoys. In Scapa Flow we always topped up with ammo. And oil. And did any repairs, because quite a lot of damage was done by heavy seas, and the sides would be dented. An aircraft carrier was never built to be a sea-faring boat.

There was always leave. My mother never knew I was coming. *I* never knew I was coming. From Scapa Flow you'd get the train down to

Perth – Edinburgh – Glasgow, then the Glasgow boat over home. It took you maybe three days travelling, and the same going back.

The ship I was on was nowhere near the Bismarck when she was sunk, but our aircraft kept tabs on her. There were two of them – the Hipper, a heavy cruiser, escort to the Bismarck, and the Bismarck herself. We were up around Greenland – we'd already passed Iceland.

When the Hood was sunk I told people – no – I'm a big fella. It doesn't worry me. But it did.

SAMUEL JOHN LESLIE
1901–1967

Conversation with Marion Hiddleston (daughter) and
Aileen McGarrigle (granddaughter)

Aileen: I think the active
service for which he finally
received the Arctic Star was as
Coxswain on HMS Norfolk –
he was up near Bear Island –
not on convoy duty as such, but
patrolling all around Bear
Island for U-boats.

Marion: Anything I heard was through my mother. He didn't talk
about it. I remember him saying that if you took your gloves off and
touched the rigging, it ripped the skin off your hands.
But he never really mentioned it while he was alive. He was a very
unassuming man. He didn't look for any rewards. We were beginning
to give up trying to get him recognition, when we enlisted the help of
John Pudney in the Limavady Museum, a member of the Royal Naval
Association. He was a great help in obtaining the posthumous medal
the Arctic Star.

No – it's not often mentioned in the story of Northern Ireland. Except that the U-boats came in and surrendered in Lough Foyle, in Londonderry.

Aileen: They've recently unveiled a big new statue to honour sailors on the Atlantic Convoys.

My grandfather had tattoos, and my daughter Heather was interested in those. She has a lot of material and photographs online. She received a letter from my uncle, where he talks about how my grandfather, who was bedaubed with tattoos, had said *Don't do it. If you are ever 'on the run' they will have a good description of you.*

Marion: My father was in the Battle of the Bismark, but the ship got damaged and they were sent back home.
He did see the Hood sinking. He knew some of the people on it. It really upset him. I was only a child at the time and he didn't really talk about it. But we were living in Devonport, Plymouth, and everyone around was associated with it. Nearly everyone knew someone on board. Officially it was played down at the time for the sake of morale.

My father joined the Navy in WWI – as a boy – then came out for a while. But it was the Depression and there was nothing else doing.

I don't believe he went ashore in Russia – those big ships didn't – but he did go ashore in the US. He was able to visit his sister there. And he was in Australia – all over the world.

Aileen: He was on different ships – and at different times was inside the Arctic Circle a lot, scooting about.

Marion: When I was a child he was away on his Far Eastern trip – he was away for three years. I don't think they do that now. I remember Fergie complaining that Prince Andrew was away so much. I think she felt it contributed to their break-up. But he was never away three years. Mother had three of us to cope with. They wrote a lot of letters, and sent a lot of those wee black-and-white photographs, showing how the children were growing up while he was away. My mother was a terrific letter writer. She had lovely hand-writing and wrote very interesting letters – very fluent. Dad was all right – they did keep in touch, but mother's letters were wonderful.

I remember once when we were living in Devonport – we were being bombed at the time. We were in the air-raid shelter almost every night. There was a knock, and we thought it was someone needing in to the shelter – that happened if anyone was caught out on the street, you would bring them in. There was a knock – and it was him, home unexpectedly. I was about ten – 1940.

Aileen: Bear Island – I had a good map. The U-boats would sneak around it. It was a big worry.

Marion: I suppose the men don't want to say the unspeakable…some things better left buried.

Churchill was very hard He did know he was sending them into serious danger, but I suppose Russia really put him under pressure. He had to give up a lot to get their help.

That photograph – my father mentioned that your skin would peel off and you had to keep your head and ears covered. They must have been slipping along, because the water would be coming over in huge waves and freezing on the spot.
But he didn't seem to want to pass on the horror to us.

They must all have lost friends and people they knew.

He was very modest. He never boasted at all. He was very quiet.
My mother would have travelled, but he said *I've done all the travelling I ever want to do.* He had a whole bookcase of *Encyclopaedia Britannica* – that was what he used to read.

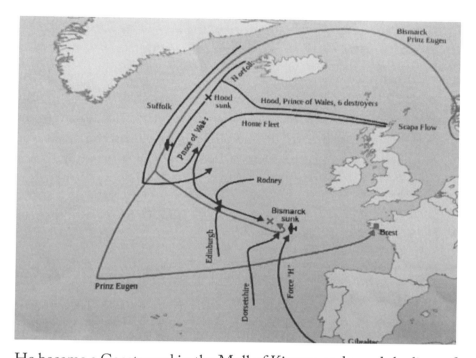

He became a Coastguard in the Mull of Kintyre and saved the lives of everyone on the Byron Darnton which ran aground off Sanda island. It was an American ship – it would have been 1946. He saw the warning light from the ship and telephoned through to Campbeltown lifeboats. Nobody lost their lives. They were all taken off the rocks. The fishermen must have gathered up…there must have been material on the ship, because there was a little row of houses, and they all had curtains the same – every house had curtains made of this material. Another girl had lots of silver cutlery from the Byron Darnton. She didn't want her stepmother to see it, so she would send it to her aunt in Glasgow – she wanted it to be safe. It probably wasn't legal at all. Just little fishing boats collecting…

We moved often in my childhood. We were in Coleraine, then my father joined up again and we all moved to Plymouth because my mother wanted to be closer to him. That was from 1938 to 1941. We were there for three years, but Dad came home on leave. We were being bombed – getting up two or three times a night to get into the shelter, and he was worried for us. He ordered my mother to come back to Northern Ireland. Then he was coastguard on the Mull of Kintyre. And finally in Bangor, County Down.

As a child I was from pillar-to-post. I had to do my 11+ three times. I got it the first time, but I had to re-sit because the next school wouldn't accept that examination board. I went to Coleraine High School.

So much is lost, really, from generation to generation. I wish I'd asked my mother – or written it down – or something.

The men must have been traumatised.

I was surprised that the War Office, who had his Naval records, didn't give him the Arctic medal. We had to fight for it. We were successful, but it's sad dad didn't know anything about it – well, he may – we don't know everything. I was eligible because I was the eldest child. I assumed my brother would be the one entitled, especially as he was in the Navy, but his sons aren't that interested. I was prepared to let them have it. I see people are selling the medals backwards and forwards online. That's really insulting, I think.

I don't know why the British didn't want to acknowledge Arctic service. Perhaps because of Russia and the Cold War – everything down to expediency.

Aileen: I've read that Britain was shipping out brand new planes to Russia, while their own airforce was making do with older models. And some of the men on the boats weren't getting rations themselves, though they were delivering supplies to Russia. But I think the Russian people who had first-hand experience of the men's bravery – they would have known the hardship and would have appreciated it.

Churchill had to sacrifice *some* people. He's bound to have thought it over and over. No wonder he was depressed. He's bound to have had nightmares.

Ship's Name	List and No.	Rating	From	To	Cause of Discharge

Marion: My mother was meticulous in terms of grammar and punctuation – she always picked up errors – 'me and my friend' would have driven her nuts.

I don't know if my father could swim. A lot of them didn't want to. They wanted to go quickly. Even nowadays, fishermen think like that. Aileen is a very strong swimmer. I've seen her swim out so far, she's like a dot.

Aileen: Not any more though. I know what they mean about the sea taking you – it's irrelevant if you can swim. I swam out from Dingle once – to swim with the dolphin – and swam very far out. I didn't know that there was a terribly strong current that swept you right out to Newfoundland – nothing between. At least I had a wet-suit on, but I was utterly exhausted. I had to get rescued by a boat. I had lost the use of my limbs, so they just landed me over the side like a kipper – I was covered in bruises. Never again.

Marion: They put up with a lot in those days – the men. I suppose it was discipline. My father spoke of very harsh discipline in the Navy. When he was a Boy Rating he lost his naval cap and he was beaten – in the Boy Navy. I don't know if it was flogging, or what method, but beaten for losing his cap.

Another time – a senior officer (senior to my father) was speaking harshly to someone under my father's command. My father intervened and spoke up in defence of the man. He was severely chastised – and demoted for doing so. He had a great sense of justice, my father, but it didn't always fit in with the Navy's strict discipline.

———

In 2003 Marion wrote of the family's time in Plymouth

We settled in well, but within a year or two, war was declared, and as we had the Naval dockyard nearby, our area soon became a target for German bombers.

Night after night, my mother had to get us out of bed, see that we had warm coats and blankets, and get us into the air-raid shelter.
During the day, we went to school. I had to go by train and carried my gas-mask, with a bar of chocolate and two digestive biscuits, which we were allowed to eat if we had to remain in the school shelter for more than two hours! We also brought our own lunches.

At the beginning of 1940, my mother had another baby. Soon after this there was an epidemic of diphtheria, and unfortunately my brother became very ill; luckily he survived, although about one third of his class didn't.

The bombing continued, night and sometimes day as well. Streets around our house were flattened, and the blasts had some strange effects, such as a picture hanging on a wall, when the rest of the house had crumbled.

Food was rationed, fuel scarce, Christmas was coming, and we were all worried about Dad, as he was on minesweepers trying to protect convoys to and from America and Russia.

One evening, during an air-raid warning, there was a knock on the door. Occasionally a passer-by would ask to share the shelter until the 'all-clear' went, so mother opened the door, and to our joy – there was dad!! He must have been given compassionate leave.
We were all so happy, nothing else mattered.

JOSIAS THOMPSON SPENCE
1906–1978

Conversation with his son, Alan Spence

I remember my father telling me about the unfriendliness of the Russians, of arriving in Archangel and a guard preventing them from leaving the pier.

He was mentioned in Dispatches in June 1944, which meant he wore an oak leaf. He survived four occasions when the ship he was on sank, and I'm not sure for which event he was honoured in this way. Two of those occasions were on the Russian Convoys.

After the war – about 1946, he used to broadcast on BBC Home Service. I remember as a child being told – *take that battery to be charged – daddy's on the radio tonight* – and vaguely I remember listening to his voice on the radio.

Since his death, I found out things he never knew, like the U-boat (U 160) that torpedoed the ship he was on. And I found the name of the German U-boat Commander in charge – Georg Lassen.

My father was born in Belfast in 1906. His mother was from Monaghan, and his father was caretaker of the old Boys' Model School. He was brought up by his aunt, and left school when he was fourteen. He was a butcher, and was married in 1935. In 1939, when war broke out, his wife had just given birth to my sister. He enlisted in the Royal Navy. My parents, within themselves, were very private.

I was born in 1941, and it was 1945 when I first met my father. I feared him. I think a lot of servicemen had lived on adrenalin for six years. They came home to a country fit for heroes that didn't actually exist.

He trained on HMS Caroline in Belfast and HMS President in Portsmouth. He was a gunner on a DEMS – a Defensively Equipped Merchant Ship, beginning as Ordinary Seaman and working his way up to Petty Officer. He kept the guns working. He fired 4.6 inch deck guns as well as Bofors guns and Oerlikons.

He was on board the Port Phillip, which was carrying a cargo of aerial bombs, when Japanese midget submarines entered Sydney Harbour and torpedoed another ship anchored nearby, which was a terrifying experience, since eighteen people were killed. He was one of a very few survivors from the Star when it was sunk off Albany, Australia.

By the KING'S Order the name of
Temporary Acting Petty Officer
Josias Thompson Spence,
D/JX 194817
was published in the London Gazette on
8 June 1944
; mentioned in a Despatch for distinguished service.
I am charged to record
His Majesty's high appreciation.

First Lord of the Admiralty

His own account of surviving a second time, when on 21st November 1942 the Dutch Merchant Ship Bintang was sunk in the Atlantic, is worth quoting from, since it is revelatory about the discipline and unwavering conviction that was required to survive.

Extract from the text by Josias Thompson Spence

As the vortex sucked me down, I firmly pressed my lips together and held my breath. Before long my lungs seemed as if they would burst and there was a thundering in my ears. I realised I was drowning...

When I returned to consciousness, I was floating in thick oil and surrounded by wreckage ... but five rafts were bobbing up and down. Later, we found that fifty-one of the ship's company of seventy-six had so far survived, but among the missing was my watch mate Joe. We searched everywhere in the sea about, but there were no more survivors. I was stunned ...

The raft I ended up on was made from six empty oil drums welded together, with rough wooden seats and a duckboard deck. We found twenty one-pint gin bottles full of water, wrapped in corrugated card. We had six pounds of round sea-biscuits; two one-pound tins of Horlicks tablets; twelve three-quarter-pound tins of bully beef; four one-pound tins of cooked tongue; nine tins of condensed milk and four pounds of slab chocolate; two woollen blankets; a dozen hand flares and a torch with batteries...On board were three Dutch officers, two Australian Engineers, three British gunners, three Javanese, and the ship's carpenter, who was a Mohammedan ...

It was fortunate that we decided to go on the shortest rations immediately, otherwise I doubt if any of us would have been alive today. Because of our immersion in the water, we were completely covered in oil, and consequently suffered from temporary blindness. The sun and the salt water caused us excruciating pain…Our water ration was about one eggcup full. I bathed my eyes and let the precious fluid trickle down onto my tongue.

We rigged awnings with the blankets to shelter us from the sun. This helped to allay our craving for water, though at all times a cup of cold water was the compass of all our desires.

Because of the survivors on one of the other rafts, who had consumed their water and were hoping to seize ours, we had to leave quietly in the middle of the night…

At night, we circulated the blankets to cover us. At regular intervals when darkness fell we flashed SOS with the torch… When we swam, we had to be very careful of sharks…

Those who ate fish seemed to become more thirsty, so we abandoned that idea…

And then our raft becalmed in the doldrums….

I found in the dark of night, that I had to keep flogging my memory – snatches of Omar Khayyam, Shakespeare, Lewis Carroll…

A wind rose and we were hit by the tail-end of a hurricane – and it was night time…

On the fourth day, 25th November 1942, we sighted a ship….

Breakfast consisted of our eggcup full of water, but with a dash of condensed milk and half an ounce of corned beef, mixed with biscuit – one good mouthful…

There was a high sea and visibility was poor, but we lit a flare ... The plume of smoke moved steadily across the horizon, and by 11 am it was out of sight ...
We were suffering from salt-water ulcers – the cuts and bruises were inflamed by fuel oil, salt water and tropical sun, and these became septic. You had to keep bathing them with sea water ... Our feet became swollen ... During the entire seventeen days, not one of us had a bowel movement due to the lack of food ...

The temperature during the day could be as high as 100 degrees, but at night it was very cold ...
A careful watch was kept to see that all got an equal share of food and water ...

On 1st December, we saw another plume of smoke. We burned two more of our precious flares, and in anticipation of rescue, we consumed the remainder of our water. We were only two miles away from the ship, and were positive that we had been seen ... But she altered course and stood away from us ... Finally we realised that we were forced back on our own resources. But this time it was hopeless – our water was finished. But the Dutch Chief Engineer had withheld a bottle, and he reckoned we had enough condensed milk to add to the water to last for a few days, and that it looked like rain...We kept on paddling.

Though we were trying to keep a log of where we were and how far we were travelling each day, I gave up hope of ever seeing my wife and children again ... I began to carve out a record of the whole business on one of the wooden paddles and each night, to fight depression, one person would recount the story of his life.

On Decemeber 4th, our water and condensed milk practically finished, the rains came. We filled the empty bottles and the empty bully tins as well … A new menace struck us – convulsions – caused by lack of certain salts which had been lost to us by evaporation … I lapsed into a stupor and dreamt continuously.

December 6th a strong gale arose, and we thought the raft would turn over. We lay that night like a lot of cattle in a stall and were terrified by the heavy seas that washed over us.

December 7th A beautiful day – and I said *Well boys, this is the day!* and was immediately sorry. Sunset came and no ship …
The rain came and at 9pm I took over my turn at the paddle. My hip bones were very painful. A dark object rose two hundred yards away. I shouted *A submarine – or a ship! Lads, get the flare!* We blew our whistles and lit our last flare. It was a large motor ship and it came very near to running us down. A voice in the broadest Scots accent called out, *Who are ye?*

We were too weak to hold onto the ropes, so they took us on tow, but I know the feelings of the condemned when they are reprieved …

It's nice to wake up after a horrid dream and realise that 'God's in his heaven and all's well with the world once again.'

THOMAS JESS
1923–2015

Tommy Jess was born in Ballykeel in Dromore, County Down in 1923. Before joining the Navy in 1942, he worked in Mackey's Engineering Company in Belfast. In 1944 he was on board one of the ships which escorted the American troops to Omaha Beach for the D-Day invasion.

He was part of the Arctic Convoys – sailing from Scotland to Iceland, and then to Murmansk.
His ship, the HMS Lapwing, was torpedoed by a German submarine, U-968.

As Laura Graham-Brown, Tommy's granddaughter says: *Being reared on a farm, my grandfather always carried a knife, and he was able, with that knife, to cut the rope tying the raft to the sinking ship ... My grandfather was very lucky. He knew that all his life.*

Transcript extracted from an interview with Thomas Jess by Richard Parkinson, recorded on 5th September 2005, for the WWII archive of the Somme Heritage Centre and Museum, Newtownards

After the Richmond, I was in Devonport and I joined HMS Lapwing, a bird-class sloop – submarine hunting. They were all named after birds: Starling, Lark, Magpie.

I was on an Oerlikon gun on the starboard side of the bridge.

We'd been on a couple of Russian convoys, and we were taken into Milford Haven in Wales. We knew something was coming up, but we didn't know what. There was a rumour going all the time, about a Second Front being opened. We weren't allowed ashore. The Captain cleared the lower deck and said *A Second Front is about to be opened.*

There was a lot of youngish fellas – maybe it was their first ship. They were terrified. I had seen a bit of service…you were able to puff and blow it a bit. I never did – but there were some who weren't very nice to the younger ones – there were bullies.

After that, there were four big American Troopers – we were sent right into France – that was really rough, really rough. It was terrible – that was the first time I saw dead bodies. That was D-Day.

From '43 to '44 it had been Arctic Convoys. They were terrible. Terrible. I would say without a doubt that Russia was the worst run. With Russian convoys you had two enemies – the cold and the real enemy.

We'd sail from Greenock. Anything up to thirty or forty ships, maybe more. And we'd be on the outside, protecting them. It was a sight. No doubt. The first convoy to Russia, I was glad I wasn't on a merchant ship, because they've no defence whatever. They've only small arms, they're totally dependent on escort ships – and when they were hit – they went. There seemed to be no water-tight compartments like we had.

On our third Russian trip – we had a sister ship, the Lark – she got her stern blew off. But they were able to take her in tow. They towed her right into Murmansk. But I heard after that that she was unrepairable. She had to be scrapped. There were nine or ten crew killed on her – the fo'c's'le gun crew.

Escort ships were very very good protection. There were some terrible losses at the beginning – I know that from reading – but as time went on and the Germans became less offensive, things got easier. It's unfortunate that we got it in the last trip – they weren't expecting it. When the Germans attacked from the air, we were 'closed up' – Action Stations. But when *we* were hit, the only ones 'closed up' were the depth charge party. I was on the bridge at the time, just cleaning the guns.

Bang? It scared the living lights out of me. Somebody shouts *We're hit!...* I was blew about ten or twelve feet down the deck. When I looked up, all I had was – my knuckles were all skinned. I was a bit sore here-and-there. I gathered myself up and ran to Action Stations, and there was the Abandon Ship command – Every Man for Himself...That was the second trip to Russia *after* D-Day.

In the earlier convoys, I've seen plenty of action. I've seen a corvette – I was on watch duty – a corvette called Bluebell – she was hit and all you could see was one big flash on the horizon. One survivor. About one mile away maybe. She had been with us on several other convoys. A glow – the magazine went up – there was one survivor, a Petty Officer.

We never picked up survivors – it was other ships maybe, astern of us. We were ahead of the convoy mostly. I thank goodness that when *we* were hit, the Savage was allowed to stop and pick us up – even though there were submarines about.

It was mostly submarines. We were always glad of rough weather – really rough weather – we seemed to be more protected. If conditions were calm we were more prone to be attacked. With Norway being occupied, German planes would reach us from there – Ju88s, 87s, dive-bombers…As gun crews, we had to learn plane recognition. I always remember the Ju88 – she was a rare shape. Fiercesome – it would have scared you to hear them screaming.

I saw one U-boat survivor. Another ship picked him up and I remember him coming ashore blindfolded. A nice-looking fella – blondish – German. That was the only one. They'd picked up one survivor.

We'd feel depth charges – we felt them even at a distance – we'd feel the compression. I remember when we were doing training and dropped depth charges you would have seen fish coming up, and they were an awful mess – oh dear – terrible – big big fish – their innards right out of their mouths. That's how you'd have been if one had exploded near you.

I remember we were allowed to hook them aboard and the cooks used them as food. On board the ship. Fish. That was in training of course, that wasn't in action.

Depth charges – they were about two feet long, fired off the stern of the ship. And we had what they called 'hedgehogs' as well, and they'd scoot right up and down and would have blew a submarine up.
I didn't see it, but we did claim a hit on a submarine – the Skipper claimed it. I think they were quite keen to claim things – that couldn't be proven. They claimed a hit anyway.

Not so much ice – I've seen icebergs, but, in fact, we were always more concerned about ice on board the ship. There were times we had to keep training the guns all the time – you know – elevating them and depressing them – keeping them working – keep them from freezing up.

Very very cold. If you had touched a hand rail, your hand would have stuck to it. The weather was so bad many a time, we weren't allowed on the upper deck. You couldn't have went up on deck, the wind, the storm, the waves were so bad they covered the whole ship nearly.

I never thought I wouldn't survive a storm. The only time I thought – when the ship was hit – I thought I was a gonner. To be honest.

The waves were powerful – but we were glad. We weren't attacked as much. There was nothing you could do in that weather. You were assigned to do different things, but you were within safety. If you went to go onto the deck, you'd have been lost. They had a way of hooking you onto the rail. I was never, but other fellas, were hooked on – only when doing emergency things.

SICK QUARTERS   "H.M.S. DRAKE."   Attending Card

RUM AND LEAVE NOT ALLOWED.	Date 14 . 5 ., 1945		
Mess	Name	Age	Rating
	JESS. T.		A B

Complaint — *Swelling of feet.*
Exposure to cold 2 hours in arctic.

DATE

Excused swimming.

G. A. Hawkins

SWIMMING BATH,
1 4 MAY 1945
R.N. BARRACKS
DEVONPORT.

Russia – we were allowed ashore into Kola. But before that the Germans had advanced right up there – everything was devastated. Everything was flattened. They were eating – the bread was black, whatever sort of food it was.

We got a lot of souvenirs and that – you had to exchange some part of your clothes, you know, for souvenirs and things like that. I brought a hammer and sickle home and it disappeared. My mother didn't like it at all. She said it was an awful thing – Communists.

The Russians were suspicious. We were warned not to drink ashore – not to get into trouble, not to argue with anybody. There was a story – I think it was true, too, that there was British sailors attacked, but they brought it on themselves probably – oul liquor – maybe drinking oul vodka or something. We had never...our Skipper commended us for being so good ashore. We always came back in one piece, and never got into any bother.

Where we were in Russia was more of a village. A lot of ships. I remember a lot of women working, whereas the men would be doing the jobs here, there'd be women doing them there – operating cranes and all there, taking the stuff off the merchant ships. You wouldn't have known them from men.

Everything was secretive. Of course, you couldn't have talked to them. Every time we went there nearly, we got ashore. But each time we were warned. They were pleasant – they all smiled at you – if you treated them all right, they were all right to you. If you were – I think there were some fellas went ashore – you know – as if they were big chief – maybe a lot of liquor in them or something...

The supplies we took out was locomotives, guns…far more than what we got back. I think it was timber and stuff we got back mostly. It wasn't much talked about. But I noticed we never were attacked as much coming back as we were attacked going. They tried to stop the supply line going *to* Russia. It wasn't very long to unload there – a lot of days just. I was glad enough to leave – well you'd be looking forward to maybe a few days at home.

———

We were involved with D-Day. After D-Day, the Germans fought back…Then we were taken back onto convoys to Russia. We'd done a convoy, then I think we got a boiler clean, so we got leave, and then we came back and picked up another convoy. That was the last one.

1945 March 20th, I remember that. Everything went very well – the usual bad weather, the usual buzzes going about submarines and all – 'til we – in fact I thought we were home and dry – right into Kola Bay. In Kola Bay there were submarines sitting waiting. I did think the war was coming to an end, then on March 20th '45 coming into Kola Bay there was this massive explosion, and everything shook – the whole ship shook from stern to bow – you know – and there was so many people running around and shouting – there was so many – the ship's doctor he was going about – there was a lot of people lying moaning and he was injecting them and that – you know.

I gathered myself up and I didn't know what to do – and then there were so many – everybody running here and there – in fact, Donald saw his best friend – mowed down – hit – just beside him. Right before his very eyes saw him blew to pieces.

I thought – with the Lark getting hit [before] – I thought 'I wonder now are we all right. Will we stay afloat?' – you know – maybe – with water-tight compartments. You see the Lark was sunk with what you call an 'acoustic torpedo' – the screws of the ship attract the torpedo, and it hits the stern and the stern's blew off, but with water-tight compartments, a ship could stay afloat. But we got it right amidships. I could feel me – where I was standing – getting further and further up – I said 'My goodness the ship's listing terrible…' Everybody was trying to get the rafts and all dismantled and all. Most of the life-boats were shattered and useless, so next thing I heard *Abandon Ship – Everyone for himself, Every man for himself.*

I jumped – oh I don't know how far – must have been – oh, the height of this house – into the water, and I didn't come up … I'd my lifebelt on – I didn't know – my best friend – it was one of the ones you blow up – it wasn't like the ones they have now, like – it was like a tube – and that was my best friend at sea. I never was a strong swimmer and I never got even taking my boots off. Sea boots and thick socks inside them and all your heavy clothes – I jumped in …

The lifebelt was blew up – always. I had it on, or always beside me – even if I was in the hammock I always kept it handy, always blew up and checking it all the time. Of course, they told you that. And some of the boys had none. But I always had mine. That's what saved my life.

And then I jumped and when I came up I spied this raft you see, and somebody said *There's a line!* Somebody was on it already, and there was a line attached to the ship from it. And I had a knife down here – in my pocket. I always carried that knife at sea. I cut the line. The line was about an inch thick and I had to saw it and saw it 'til I got it off.

So we got away and we tried to – a couple of the boys pulled me onto the raft – and by-the-way it wasn't a normal raft, it was a carley raft. There was twelve of us – I think twelve on the one raft. Seven of us were picked up after about two hours or more.

You see it's a net bottom – you're in the water when you're in it – but you're in the net – it's a carley raft. The water was very cold, very cold. After a while you just went numb. They reckon, when they picked Donald up – they had to pull the rope…it was either break his fingers or pull the rope. They pulled the rope and all the skin came off – the rope was right through his hand. He had a 'death grip'. He had a 'death grip' holding on. They reckon…they don't know where they went to: there was twelve of us on the raft, only seven picked up. The seventh one – they worked on him on board the Savage – the destroyer that picked us up, but he died. They worked on him but they couldn't do nothing for him. I always remember his name – a fella called Biddle from Birmingham. A big blondie-haired fella. They buried him at sea.

When the ship went down – we were concerned – the suckage. We always knew about that if a ship went down. But it was enough to get away. The last thing I saw was a wee bit of the bow – just a wee bit of the bow sticking up – I remember….

The screams of the men below'll haunt me for the rest of my days…

We could do nothing for them.

You see – when the ship – all the hatches were jammed, and they couldn't get out you know. So we could hear them screaming.

Speech of the Russian Ambassador A. Yakovenko at the Ceremony of awarding Ushakov medal to Arctic convoy veterans

Belfast, 31 October 2014

Dear veterans of the Arctic convoys,

Dear friends,

It is a huge privilege for me to thank you on behalf of the Russian Government for the invaluable contribution you and your comrades-in-arms made to the defeat of the Nazi Germany.

What you did 70 years ago, taking part in what Sir Winston Churchill rightly called *the worst journey in the world*, was extraordinary even among what is considered to be beyond the call of duty.

Thousands of Allied seamen lost their lives as the British ships sailed in the unwelcoming, stormy waters of the Arctic ocean under a constant threat of being attacked by German U-boats and aircraft.

Your heroism will always be remembered in Russia and Britain. Your deeds will continue to serve as the supreme expression of bravery and a high point in human spirit.

I am confident that it was not by accident that our nations found themselves on the right side of history, which the followers of the ideology of hatred wanted to stop, while depriving nations of their inalienable right to decide their destiny. The allied effort required all the best in the national spirit of the British and the peoples of the Soviet Union, the very strength of character that we are rightfully proud of.

The comradeship-in-arms, which was born at the truly critical juncture of history will forever remain an important part of European spirital heritage and our bilateral relationship, including the ties between the two navies.

On the instruction of President Vladimir Putin I have the honour of presenting to you the Ushakov medals.

Bibliography

AKHMATOVA, Anna: Selected
Poems, Translated by DM
Thomas; Penguin, London 1985.

ANTRIM GUARDIAN, 13th
November, 2014.

BROWN, Peter C.: Voices from the
Arctic Convoys; Fonthill, England
2014.

FIENNES, Ranulph: Cold; Simon
and Schuster, London 2013.

IRVING, David: The Destruction of
Convoy PQ17; St Martin's Press,
New York 1968 and 1987.

KEMP, Paul: Convoy! Drama in
Arctic Waters; Cassell & Co.,
London 1993.

KENNEDY, Ludovic: Menace. The
Life and Death of the Tirpitz;
Sphere Books, England 1981.

LISBURN STAR, 2nd October, 2015.

McAUGHTRY, Sam: The Sinking of
the Kenbane Head; Blackstaff
Press, Belfast 1977.

MacLEAN, Alistair: HMS Ulysses;
Harper Collins, 1994.

MAYNARD, Major General Sir C.:
The Murmansk Venture; Naval

and Military Press Litd.,
England.

MONSARRAT, Nicholas: The
Cruel Sea; Penguin Books 1957.

ROSS, Alan: Poems; The Harvill,
London.

SCHOFIELD, Vice Admiral B. B.:
The Arctic Convoys; MacDonald
and Jane's, London 1977.

SMITH, Peter C.: Convoy PQ18
Arctic Victory; New English
Library; England 1975.

TAYLOR, Theodore: Battle in the
Arctic Seas; Sterling Publishing
Company, New York 1976.

THUBRON, Colin: In Siberia;
Chatto and Windus, London
1999.

WHEELER, Sara: The Magnetic
North; Travels in the Arctic;
Vintage Books.

WICKS, Ben: Waiting for the All
Clear – True Stories from
Survivors of the Blitz; Guild,
London 1990.

WOODMAN, Richard: The Arctic
Convoys 1941-1945; John
Murray, London 1994.